POWER HOUSE

A collection of empowering and inspiring
stories packed with business gold
from successful female entrepreneurs

Elizabeth McQuillan

SUPPORTED BY:

The PUBLISHING
POD

Copyright © 2025 by Elizabeth McQuillan

ISBN 9798310443761

All rights reserved.

No part of this book may be reproduced in any form or by any electronic or mechanical means, including information storage and retrieval systems, without written permission from the author, except for the use of brief quotations in a book review.

Contents

1. Elizabeth McQuillan — 1
Powerhouse — 4
2. Elizabeth Warburton — 19
The Power in Being Brave — 22
3. Kim Antrobus — 33
Temptress of Change — 36
4. Louise Cadman — 47
She Believed She Could, and She Did — 51
5. Lucy Anjuna — 63
Always Be the Leading Lady in Your Own Life! — 66
6. Caroline Hargreaves — 77
This is Not How My Story Ends — 80
7. Nicole Louise Geddes — 95
Show Up Like a Showgirl — 98
8. Karen Nicholson — 113
0-60 in a Chapter — 116
9. Donna Amos — 127
Seat at the Table — 130

10. Chef Seema Dalvi	143
Live Like a Goddess and Do the Right Thing	146
11. Jennifer Parker	157
Never Settle	160
12. Ann Shirley	171
Breaking the Bias	174
13. Debbie-Lyn Connolly-Lloyd	189
Dream It, Believe It, Achieve It	192
14. Amanda Shearer	203
Finding Miss Moneypenny	206
15. Rachael Hover	219
Embrace Your Uniqueness	222
16. Lindsey Fairhurst	229
Live Life by DESIGN, Not Default	232
17. Louisa Herridge	245
On the Other Side of Fear	248

POWERHOUSE

Elizabeth McQuillan

About the Collaboration Host

Elizabeth McQuillan is a serial entrepreneur and franchisor, Elizabeth owns Flamingo Car Finance, Flamingo Business, Flamingo Business Awards and has a property portfolio.

She is passionate about demystifying jargon and empowering people with knowledge across her businesses, helping clients scale their business or purchase their dream car.

Elizabeth is an advocate for building success from nothing and believes that everyone, regardless of race, gender, or age, possesses the attributes of a POWERHOUSE.

Elizabeth was a teacher for fourteen years before leaving this career to build a finance brokerage with her husband, Phil. This transition happened two weeks before lockdown of COVID hit, requiring resilience and determination to keep both the family and business afloat during challenging times.

Within three months, the company was writing six figures per month in finance – an incredible turnaround!

She is a mum to Ruby and Loretta, step mum to Bella and Benj, wife to Phil, and a dog mum to Baily dog!

Together we rise!

Email: ladies@flamingocarfinance.co.uk

Website: www.flamingobusiness.co.uk

Website: www.flamingocarfinance.co.uk

Powerhouse

Let me ask you a question... Do you class yourself as a Powerhouse?

A Powerhouse by definition is:

'A person or thing of great energy, strength, or power.'

Does this resonate with you?

I believe 100% that I AM A POWERHOUSE!

I am a person of great energy...

I have strength...

I have power...

And, without a shadow of doubt, I truly believe that everything that I encompass: my core values, my mission, my beliefs, what I represent, inertly leans into this word: POWERHOUSE.

I also believe that, with the right mindset, anyone, regardless of gender, race, or age, contains attributes of a Powerhouse and this is why I have brought together sixteen women to showcase exactly this. These women have businesses in all different niches and have come from varied backgrounds and all showcase energy, strength, and power.

Now let me ask you this...

Are you born a Powerhouse, or are you made a Powerhouse?

It is the common nature versus nurture question. Are we born this way or are we made this way because of life experiences?

Let me take you back to the summer of 1996.

Have you ever experienced a nosebleed? Maybe a trickle, maybe a snuffle? But have you ever experienced a nosebleed that is so forceful that it gushes from your nose and mouth with clots of blood that continues for over two hours?

Have you ever woken up with a bruise, unsure of where it's come from? (Let's face it, this usually happens following a good night out on the town!) But imagine being eleven years old and having a body covered with unexplained bruises and a pin prick rash.

Let's add to this: utter exhaustion from performing on stage in a routine dance which results in you collapsing at the side of the stage in total fatigue. Not the behaviour you'd expect from a supposedly healthy, eleven-year-old!

It was this biological deficient overload, that lead to my mum taking me to the doctors, that gloomy morning in May 1996.

Within hours, I was 'blue-lighted' to The Royal Manchester Children's Hospital and told that I had an extremely rare blood disorder. One that required an urgent bone marrow transplant. If a member of my immediate family wasn't a perfect match, I didn't have long enough to live, whilst an international bone marrow search was undertaken.

In those desperate moments – I was a far cry from a Powerhouse.

Thankfully my eldest sister, Lianne, was a perfect bone marrow match and was the hero of my story and the rest is history. I fought off a life-threatening disease with the help of my sister, and it was in that moment where I believe that my Powerhouse journey began.

Looking back at that time in my life makes me want to live every day as though it's my last. My outlook now is that trivial things do not stop me on my journey or bring me down. I have a level of gratitude where even the simplest of things like breathing in that cool, crisp winter air, brings me more happiness than I dare to dream, knowing that my life could have ended at age eleven.

Powerhouse: Born.

Some people will believe that we are made Powerhouses because of turbulent pasts. There is definitely a strong correlation between those who have risen like the phoenix through the ashes and are now a burning reflection of all things POWERHOUSE!

Overcoming adversity strengthens our Powerhouse attributes and, when it comes to ticking the adversity boxes, there's not many that I haven't ticked!

From facing death as a child to unexpectedly having the rug pulled from under my feet back in 2015 when, as a thirty-year-old mummy, I was forced to move back into my parent's box room, sharing a room AND bed with my two-year-old daughter, after her father left under the cloud of multiple affairs.

Powerhouse: Activated.

But the next part of my journey, took me from Powerhouse activated, to Powerhouse: AMPLIFIED!

Now, are you sitting comfortably? I'm about to take you on a journey back to 2020...

'Let's just get through this alive!'

These words were said on repeat during the dreaded and feared early days of lockdown.

The words were said repeatedly by all around me, who flooded me with words of support and love. You see, I'd found my knight in shining armour! Not only was he loving, supportive, successful – and devilishly handsome – he also understood me and believed in me. Our relationship wasn't just based on love, we were about to partner in business too. In fact, it was all just a little bit, 'too good to be true!'

Following a fourteen-year career as a teacher, I was about to take the brave leap of faith into full entrepreneurial life and head up our new car finance company, Flamingo Associates.

This was our business baby – an extension of Phil's current business in the automotive industry – a finance brokerage.

I had no previous experience of this industry, in fact, I'd been 'that girl' who'd walked into the bright lights and shiny floored dealership and had been descended upon by a flock of vultures, with unguarded pound signs, flooding the proximity as they burst the banks of their bulging eyes.

Yes, I'd been 'car salesmen'd' numerous times before now, but little did I realise that this would serve me well in the future…

We'd planned the launch of the new business, meticulously. I was to leave my fourteen-year career as a teacher on Friday, to be whisked off to the Maldives to marry my prince on the Sunday and to return as full time marital and business partners. I'd even had my wedding dress chosen by Gok Wan and appeared on TV in 'Say Yes to the Dress.'

I mean, come on… this was what fairy tales were made of.

But two weeks before, the unimaginable happened!

'Do not leave your house, do not pass go, do not collect £100.'

Yes, Boris announced full country lockdown and the dream wedding plans disappeared in a millisecond!

Twelve months of plans scrapped in a blink of an eye. But rather than having a complete meltdown, I stayed strong and prayed that we would all 'get through this alive!' The fear of death outweighed the sadness of the wedding cancellation.

I diligently emailed my head teacher to discuss options of retracting my resignation, but, to my despair, this was rejected as a new teacher had already been contracted!

I was left jobless and heartbroken as my idyllic dreams had crumbled to the floor.

So... what does a Powerhouse do when faced with adversity?

THEY POWER THROUGH!

Yes, I picked myself up, I dusted myself off and, like the mouse who fell in the milk, I churned the milk into cheese so I could climb out of the danger zone.

Every morning, without fail, I got up, got dressed and hit the kitchen (my new office). I had been building the finance brokerage infrastructure quietly in the background and now was the time to launch!

I positioned this lockdown adversity as the bow and arrow analogy. The bow must be pulled backwards, before it shoots forward, with speed and determination. The pullback came as a surprise, we can't deny this, however, the release of the string created the most incredible arrow thrust you could have ever imagined!

Within three months, I was single-handedly bringing in six figure months! This was WILD! I remember Phil looking at our accounts and asking me what strategy I was following, telling me that, whatever it was, to keep doing it.

Within eighteen months, we'd written our first £1,000,000, which then went on to increase to £4,000,000 in year three.

So, what had I done?

- I'd enlisted the assistance of a business mentor.
- I'd turned my pain into power and leaned into my passion for community to create a following of loyal buyers.
- I'd positioned myself as the 'Go-To Expert,' in car finance, niching into helping women.

My mission was to 'demystify the jargon,' empowering females with the knowledge to help them make an independent, financial decision.

I had been the clueless car buyer – now I was set to help similar people with similar problems.

I grew my audience quickly online and rebranded using bright pinks and a flamingo. It was unique to my industry. It was eye catching, attention grabbing and relatable for women.

I would look forward to a Sunday evening when an online business owner would open a new Facebook group and jump in to networking like a ninja, dropping my staple introduction into the thread. Connecting with others, initiating new conversations, and building a strong 'know, like, trust' across the social media platforms.

I read countless books on marketing and sales and tracked my customer journey, segmenting it into seven Key Result Areas:

1. Prospecting.

2. Building Rapport.

3. Identifying Needs.

4. Presenting the Sale.

5. Handling Objections.

6. Closing.

7. Referrals.

I studied Dr William Moulton Marston & Thomas Erikson theories of DISC personality types and became obsessed. I used this knowledge to help me understand my clients and the ways they preferred to be communicated with, in a sales environment. I later turned this into a comprehensive training session, helping other entrepreneurs with their SALES systems.

I created numerous other business trainings that would help business owners with their revenue generating strategies, whilst turning up, day after day, online to grow, educate, entertain, and nurture my audience.

When the time came for lockdown restrictions to be lifted, I attended countless in-person events constantly growing my audience, and, after tracking lead generation and conversion stats within the company, it was clear that networking was the key catalyst to all our sales. It was the no. 1 marketing strategy that was bringing in the highest ROI.

Enter Company Number 2 – Flamingo Business

After the COVID cloud of 2020 lifted, we eloped to Mykonos to recreate our cancelled wedding. We beat numerous odds in our pursuit for happiness, including an ectopic pregnancy and ovary/fallopian tube extraction to conceive our miracle, rainbow baby whilst basking in the sun.

During the Christmas period of 2021, I put a post on social media, asking if anyone wanted to have dinner with me, inviting them to share a table with me whilst I discussed the steps I'd taken to create such fast growth in the business. This post generated significant interest, as one hundred women jumped in my DMs wanting to buy my first 'Flamingo Business Experience' ticket!

Since that day, I have helped hundreds of women, from across the globe, grow their business through the power of networking and in-person connection. In fact, statistically, 82% of any business, regardless of industry, is generated through in-person connection or referral.

I have hosted quarterly in-person business events since that first experience back in 2021, along with monthly networking events in the Northwest of England. The company has subsequently created and sold numerous franchises of this business model, and in November 2024 we held the inaugural Flamingo Business Awards which, without doubt, was one of the proudest businesses moments, to date.

As a Powerhouse, I leaned into my strengths of leading; connecting and uplifting others thus creating ripples of impact. This also helped create new revenue streams for the business, whilst acting as a lead generation to our finance company – Golden!

So, let's come back to the question I asked at the beginning of this chapter:

Are we born a Powerhouse, or is it something we become as a result of our life experiences – shaped by both the highs and the lows?

I'll leave this to your own interpretation, but what I will say is this:

WE ARE ALL POWERHOUSES!

From serial entrepreneur to full time mummy…

Regardless of our role, or the path we have taken in life, we are all, 'people of great energy, strength, or power.'

Our paths aren't often straightforward with many twists and turns along the way, but undeniably, there are many moments in our lives that have required us to have the **energy** to start, the **strength** to continue and the **power** to see it through!

I see you.

I admire you.

I cheer you!

As part of my mission to connect and inspire more entrepreneurs I have brought together Powerhouse business owners who will all be sharing their Powerhouse stories and business gold. Alongside the power of stories, I want you to learn something from each author so at the end of each chapter you will be gifted some delicious business gold. So, before I hand over to my incredible co-authors, I wanted to share with you some of my own business gold that I use to help scale my businesses.

Powerhouse Business Gold

1. Position yourself as a Key Person of Influence! This will help speed up your customers to 'know, like, trust – buy'! The best way to become a KPI is to share value, in rooms full of your ideal clients! Or even better... create your own room of ideal clients (ask me about partnering with me as a Flamingo Business franchisee: DM me on Instagram @flamingobusiness_)

2. Mindset is the driving force of all you achieve. You become what you think you are capable of. So, think BIG! Be audacious with your goals. Keep your mindset strong and positive, and watch the results roll in.

3. Strive for financial independence – this will bring about unwavering confidence.

4. Passion and determination will top trump any qualification or IQ.

5. Back yourself: financially and energetically.

6. Remember – you are in control of your own destiny!

Very few have things handed to them on a plate… you will get out of life what you put into life.

7. Control what you can – let go of the things you can't.

8. Remember that fear is not a tangible object, it's an emotion. Face it head-on! On the opposite side of fear is either progress, happiness, or a lesson that you can learn from.

9. Work smart – not hard.

10. Lean into your productivity hours – if 5am feels productive for you – exploit it! Trying to function at a time in the day where you are flagging will be counterproductive.

11. Grow multiple revenue streams, including a monthly recurring one.

12. Have making impact your driving force and the income will follow.

13. Build assets within your business, the more assets the more desirable and valuable your company will be.

14. Always remember your 'WHY.' We work to live, not live to work… Peak performance includes an equal quadrant of: self, family, health, wealth.

15. Finally – be like the Flamingo and:

Stand tall,

Stand proud,

Stand out.

If this book has ignited your desire to achieve more, be more, and have more, I'd love to support you! Whether it's through business mentoring, networking opportunities, or even starting a new business, let's make it happen. Partner with us and set up a Flamingo Business franchise in your area! Follow me on Instagram and DM the word 'Flamingo' for a complimentary 20-minute strategy call.

Or if it's time for a new car... let's empower you with the knowledge you need to make that independent, financial decision and purchase your dream car!

POWERHOUSE

Elizabeth Warburton

About the Author

Elizabeth, founder of Alchemist Yoga, is an award-winning Health and Wellness Warrior who empowers individuals to transform their health, find balance and rediscover purpose. Before starting her wellness business, Elizabeth earned a first-class honours degree in pharmacy and owned a thriving pharmacy in Lancashire for twenty years.

Now, she infuses modern science with ancient wellbeing to help individuals overcome stress, build resilience, and live a life full of joy and happiness. With over 500 hours of yoga teacher training in disciplines such as ashtanga, yin, vinyasa, philosophy, meditation, breath-work and mindfulness, her journey has taken her around the world, including India, Bali, and Ireland. She also holds numerous certifications from strength training to Pilates, HiiT to barre and serves as an Instructor Coach for Les Mills UK, mentoring instructors to bring their best to their classes.

Elizabeth lives by the coast with her soulmate, Dalmatian, and Siberian cat. She loves spending time outdoors, exploring beaches or trekking local mountains. She also has a passion for travel, music, and cooking.

Elizabeth is available for collaborations, wellness events, and retreats, as well as private and group sessions.

You can reach Elizabeth at:

Email: info@alchemist.yoga

Facebook: www.facebook.com/elizabeth.roberts.5036

Instagram: www.instagram.com/elizabeththeyogacoach

I dedicate this book to my wonderful parents, Margaret and Clifford Warburton. Everything I am today is because of the love, support and life lessons you've given me. Thank you for showing me what it means to be strong, kind and true to myself.

The Power in Being Brave

I've always found it fascinating how we measure success. As a seven-figure business owner with the big house, nice cars, long term relationship and lavish lifestyle, I was what many would describe as 'successful' but what is success? How do we define it? And is everything that we aspire to be or have really an illusion?

Reflecting on my journey, I'm reminded of Jim Carrey's words, "I think everybody should get rich or famous and do everything they ever dreamed of so they can see that it's not the answer." It took me forty-two years to realise this for myself.

Last week, during my Pilates training, a photo was captured by my very first mentor and it brought my journey full circle. From nervous student hiding at the back of the room, living a life that felt like a lie to wellness warrior living and breathing my passion and purpose. And all it took was ONE BRAVE STEP.

Sometimes we have to let go of all the things that are weighing us down to truly take flight. If I hadn't walked away from my seven-figure pharmacy business and a marriage where my identity was overshadowed, that photo wouldn't exist. Now what I see in that photo is a woman free from purgatory of perfectionism and pretension, immersing herself in knowledge she can pass on and share with others.

I now wake up every day with a zest for life. On a daily basis, I witness individuals transforming their lives through my work. As an international wellness leader, coach, presenter, and global retreat host I truly feel I have found my Ikigai.

Ikigai is a Japanese concept referring to a person's purpose or reason for living. It encourages us to discover what matters and to live a life filled with joy and purpose. The four pillars consist of: What are you good at? What do you love? What does the world need more of? and What can you get paid for? To me this is a measure of success.

Inspired by my own journey, I now blend modern science with holistic wellness to transform individuals' bodies, minds, and lives. Combining ancient practices such as yoga and meditation with evidence-based physiology and psychology I empower others to live a life of both health and happiness. With each retreat, event, coaching session, and class, I infuse the lessons I've learned and the knowledge I've gained through my personal and professional journey.

Recently I have been both humbled and honoured to receive a Health and Wellness Award for these services. This incredible moment reminded me of the transformative power of stepping back into ourselves and letting go of the facade of living for others.

The other week, I looked out into the room whilst teaching a beautiful BodyBalance™ class, with friends and students who have been with me since the start of my journey, and just breathed it all in. I saw each one of them with the burdens that they carry. Living with anxiety, self-doubt, and insecurities, lost loved ones, battles with illness, recovering from surgeries. Yet, here we all were, moving together, supporting one another in this shared space. I'm beyond grateful to provide this space where we can simply be. This space gives us the strength to recharge, so we can return to our lives feeling calmer, stronger, and ready to take on whatever comes our way.

My motto is, "Your purpose is not the thing you do... It's the thing that happens in others when you do what you do!" But how do you turn that passion into purpose?

Let's rewind to 2015. To others I looked successful, the perfect Instagram highlights life. Yes, I owned a seven-figure pharmacy business, but I dreaded every day I walked through the door. I married a pharmacist but was often made to feel like a shadow. My mortgage was paid off, but I didn't feel at home. To others I was an independent woman who had decided family life wasn't for her, but in reality, I had eight years of IVF as I was infertile. I went on exotic holidays, but each time felt sick thinking about returning back to reality. I had followed the social norm – school, university, work, and marriage. I didn't know anything different, and I certainly didn't have any life experience. I went to the same places with the same people and wore the same fake smile. The truth was the material possessions I owned really owned me. I was trapped and at the age of forty-two felt I had a millstone around my neck, no way out, was this 'success?' Was this 'life?'

I had lost my identity; I was a shell; a shadow of my former self. I was introverted and had lost all my confidence. I felt I had nothing interesting to say and nothing in common with anyone. To be honest, I felt pretty alone. I did find solace in the gym. I had always enjoyed keeping fit and healthy. From a young age I spent a lot of time walking in the Lake District and playing tennis with my family. I also loved gymnastics and athletics. However, at the gym I shied away from classes, feeling I was an imposter and kept my headphones on so nobody would talk to me. Even in this environment I felt like I didn't fit in. What was missing?

It was some six years after this that I heard the term 'narcissist.' At the time, it seemed such a toxic, harsh word, but anyone who has experienced a narcissistic relationship would understand. As an empath, I was naturally drawn to him. Empaths are more forgiving and understanding of harmful behaviours. They tend to prioritise others' needs over their own, are prone to people pleasing and struggle with low self-esteem, making them more vulnerable to having their insecurities exploited.

In 2015 my life changed. I said, "I can't do this anymore," to my husband.

We were sitting outside in the cold at yet another beer festival. I felt like all the life had been sucked out of me. He said to me, "You're not happy are you," and it just came out of me, without a thought or hesitation, "No... I can't do this anymore."

"What do you mean?" was the reply. I stuttered out, "This, relationship, this... life." The rest of that day is a blur, we walked home some twenty metres apart with him shouting all sorts of things at me, most of them completely irrelevant. Yet all the while I just felt like a weight had been lifted. Although lighter, I felt incredibly daunted by what my new future would hold. What about the five-bedroom house we lived in, the fancy cars, the expensive shoes, and holidays? I just knew they didn't make me truly happy.

During this big transition I had also changed the gym I trained at. It seemed like such a different atmosphere. Friendly, safe, and non-pretentious. I started to try a few spinning and spartan classes and found I actually had things in common with people, I felt at ease and started to talk to people.

And then came the real trajectory of my life – Les Mills BodyBalance™. It was a new class to the centre, and I fell in love with it from the very start. I hid at the back of the room, immersed in the music, the flow and space it offered me. For that hour I forgot about all my worries and fears, as though time stood still. I started to find my 'happy' and my 'self.' I also began to get compliments. "You're so strong yet graceful," and "You are an inspiration." So unused to compliments, I found them hard to take, so in true British fashion I always had a smart reply. As time went by, I became more confident, practising in the middle of the room, then at the front.

Then came another brave decision. Even though I had sold my business, I still had a tribunal to attend. A pharmacist I employed to help manage the store was taking me to court for unfair dismissal. He had been bullying a member of staff and was now trying to blackmail us for £42K. I was sat on a train going to the first day of the hearing (I won by the way!), I had just left my husband and felt completely bewildered with all these big changes to my life. For a while I had been toying with the idea to train as a BodyBalance™ instructor just to broaden my own knowledge. I logged onto the Les Mills Instructor site for the 100th time and pressed Book Training Now. I just knew it was the right decision, but at the time I didn't know what a big impact it would have on my life, and others.

After passing the certification I started to cover classes and was complimented on what an inspiration I was. How people felt so calm yet empowered in my presence.

I still had my limiting beliefs. Other instructors were 'better than me,' 'more fun than me,' 'more knowledgeable than me.' I had lived for so long in a controlling relationship, where I was told what to wear, what to do, what to think, but I now began to understand myself more, my likes and dislikes, trust my own opinion. A song in our track list, 'Bird set free,' by Sia resonated with me so much. I felt my wings had been clipped for those twenty years, but I had taken the brave steps to see if they had healed and now there I was – a bird set free.

Elizabeth's Business Gold

I am most certainly living proof that we can find our Ikigai, our purpose, at any stage of our lives and finding time on my mat helped me to do that. I found space and time away from external influences. In our fast-paced world we are constantly switched on, often in fight or flight mode. Be it through social media, our monkey minds, or stressful jobs and juggling family life. Science says we are more than our physical bodies. In yoga this can be likened to the five koshas. The physical body (muscles, bones, and organs), the energy body (breath and life force), the mental body (thoughts, emotions, and mind), the wisdom body (inner wisdom, intuition, awareness, gut feeling), and lastly our deepest layer the bliss body where we experience pure joy and connection.

Practising yoga nidra helps us work through these layers. Research shows it can activate our parasympathetic nervous system, our rest and digest, reducing cortisol (our stress hormone) and increasing GABA, which helps to reduce anxiety and depression. It guides us into a state of deep relaxation, our brain waves slow down, shifting from beta (alert) to alpha and theta (relaxed) which enhances your brain's natural healing abilities, boosts creativity and can even improve memory. It is a practice I love to share with clients and students. Be it to release tension, inspire and energise, or simply give them permission to rest.

By seamlessly blending my scientific expertise, multi-disciplinary wellness practices and dedication to empowering others, I offer more than just a class, retreat, course, or one-to-one coaching. I offer a transformative journey rooted in authenticity and compassion. I am able to provide this space for others, which I had found all those years ago. A quiet centred space where you can finally silence those external voices and find yourself again. If you feel trapped in your body, mind or life that is your internal voice screaming for you to make a change. And trust me when you do, life has a habit of suddenly pointing you in the right direction. Think about what you could do unshackled from all your problems and worries. What would you feel excited and inspired to do? What are you capable of? What could you make real for you?

My support extends far beyond the mat, inspiring and uplifting those who work with me. Empowering people to reclaim their health, renew their energy and reimagine their potential.

To me, success aligns closely with what Michelle Obama once said, "Success isn't about how much money you make, it's about the difference you make in people's lives." In yoga philosophy, Patanjali's Eight Limbs of Yoga offer a framework for living a meaningful and purposeful life. One of these limbs, the Niyamas, represents personal observances, practices that encourage self-care, mindfulness and living in line with our values.

Within the Niyamas, Santosha, or contentment stands out as a reminder to appreciate the present moment and find fulfilment in what we already have, rather than always seeking happiness in external achievements. How often do we think, "I'll be happy when..." whether it's earning more money, losing weight, or buying something new? I am truly so grateful that the brave decisions I made have led me to a place of contentment, allowing me to redefine what success truly means.

My Santosha lies in the joy of living my purpose and helping others on their wellness journeys, rather than in owning a thriving pharmacy business.

I am here to dispel the myth that yoga and holistic wellness is not just about touching your toes or balancing on one leg. When we infuse these ancient teachings with modern science it can be so much more. As I hope you can now see, so much of what we learn on the yoga mat can be integrated into our daily lives. Whether through yogic philosophy, asanas (physical poses), pranayama (breath control) or dhyana (calming the fluctuations of the mind) we can learn patience, gratitude, acceptance, strength, courage or simply find that space to just to press pause, let go of what society deems success to be and tune into what truly matters.

I am incredibly grateful to my mum and dad for the wonderful upbringing I had. The lessons learned throughout my childhood shaping me into the woman I am today and my path into pharmacy, which I now uniquely infuse with eastern wellbeing. Sadly, my mum is no longer with us after suffering a fatal stroke a few years ago. I am so grateful to be able to spend time with my dad; until you suffer a loss of a loved one you can often take it for granted that they will always be there with you in the physical sense. I do feel my mum is still with me, I held her hand as she took her last breath just as she held mine as I took my first and I also have her scribed onto my ribs. We found an envelope when she passed and written on the back was, "I hold you close within my heart, and there you will remain, to walk with me throughout my life, until we meet again." I now have her by my side until we meet again.

One of my mum's friends attends the very class I mentioned at the beginning of this chapter. I chatted to her after class and mentioned the thoughts and emotions that had risen for me during that class. She messaged me later that day, "Liz... After we'd been chatting outside the studio yesterday, I had coffee with Chris, Joy and Marjory and told them what you'd been saying. We were all very touched and moved to tears. Then seeing your beautiful words on your post enforced how right you are... it is more than a class. We have been with you since you were a member of the class, then a shy quiet pupil learning to be a Les Mills instructor and watching you emerge as able and confident but a very humble leader of our beautiful class. You are an inspiration, Liz. Your mum would be so proud of what you have achieved and the lovely life you have made for yourself. You take care, keep smiling and see you next week. Enid xx"

If I hadn't taken those brave decisions, that moment would not have existed, we wouldn't be sharing that sanctuary, and those lives wouldn't be impacted. Sometimes, the bravest decisions feel impossible in the moment, but they open doors you never even imagined could exist. Take those brave decisions, my friends. You never know just how important they'll be.

As I complete this book, my heart is heavy with loss and full of gratitude. My beloved dad, who shaped so much of who I am, sadly passed away during this process. I am deeply sorry that he never got to read it, but I dedicate it to his memory, carrying his love and wisdom with me always. May his legacy of kindness and strength inspire others through these words.

POWERHOUSE

Kim Antrobus

About the Author

Kim Antrobus is a brand and marketing strategist who helps female entrepreneurs and small business owners confidently *emerge* online, *flourish* in the online world and *thrive* in front of their ideal clients.

Before starting her business, **Totally You Creative**, Kim worked as a paralegal for twenty years, in business development for over ten years, and as a Marketing Executive since 2023. Kim also performs as a professional singer. After a successful time working in marketing and content creation, Kim identified a need for authentic marketing aligned with business owners' values and energy.

Kim now helps women to build a presence online (and in-person) with branding and marketing advice, design, and content creation that is aligned to their values as well as their brand, product, or service.

In her spare time, Kim sleeps and eats. She has four children and very little spare time!

You can reach Kim at:

Email: hello@totallyyoucreative.co.uk

Website: totallyyoucreative.co.uk

Social media: www.instagram.com/totallyyoucreative

Temptress of Change

Let me set the scene: autumn has almost passed. The trees have shed their leaves and stand nakedly bereft of their vibrancy and purpose. It is a familiar sight, and we all trust the process. Nature knows what she is doing; shedding the past, confident that better things will come again. Spring will soon saunter in (probably late as usual) with hope and its glorious renewal. The trees will reclaim their power and once again provide sustenance for others and bloom better and stronger than before.

November is usually my favourite time of year: my birthday month (party time), walking down red and gold lined streets with those discarded leaves crunching beneath my feet; the kind of fresh air that makes your face feel slapped but alive; the crackling bonfires eagerly devouring their fuel, yearning for more; the flamboyant fireworks flirting in the darkest night skies; cherishing the comfort of cosy nights in, hot chocolates and crumbles. Each year, my family get together on Bonfire Night – all eighteen of us in one place. Lots of love, laughter, chatting and cheer, and always reassuring one another *we should do this more often* (though we never do).

This year, on the eve of Bonfire Night, my world was torn apart, and my heart shattered into a million pieces. This is my story of renewal, change and growth – the art of being a temptress of change.

It is staggering how much your life can change in just twelve months. With the shadow of the indignation cruelly closing in on you, there will come a time when you realise your own mortality; life doesn't come with a guarantee. Everything we work, plan, and strive for could be gone in an instant, and yet we all fight fiercely to forge safety *for the future.* So many people worry about their pensions and investments, paying off their mortgage, and when they will be able to retire and enjoy the fruits of their labour (and intentional self-deprivation). We all waste inordinate amounts of time worrying about the dreaded *unknown.* This year, the daunting reality of life's uncertainty came storming in, without permission, and hit me square in the face like a blunt trauma – and I *reeled.* There is nothing to gain from fearing something that might never happen or fighting something which inevitably will. However, you can inadvertently close yourself off to opportunities, success, and happiness by trying to keep yourself "safe" by avoiding change.

Putting it bluntly, this uninvited and most unwelcome change did not feel safe, and my usual valour evaporated. This change was beyond my control. There was nothing I could do to change it or stop it. But I had to sit with it. I had to focus on gratitude for the things I do have and allow life to unravel before me. I decided there and then that I would stop holding back and putting "that thing" off. Procrastination is the thief of joy. (Trust me, I am an expert in procrastination!) Inaction is a *choice;* by changing nothing, we are accepting things as they are. Like those deciduous trees in autumn, you can change and not fear it; just have faith in yourself that, ultimately, you will blossom again.

I have never feared change – I was always in control of it. Change was my bitch. I have changed direction more than a tourist lost in London. Two years ago, I decided to change career. I had been a lawyer since the late nineties. I had studied Law at A-Level and university, and I had always worked in Law in some capacity or other. It wasn't even the easy, comfortable choice; it was making me ill. Not conceding to change was the same as accepting the situation. I have changed careers before, but I have always held on to Law, like Gollum and those precious rings. I am a successful international vocalist, and I have developed and run a six-figure business, both of which gave me choices, freedom, and opportunity.

At the start of 2023, I was chronically stressed, burnt out and overwhelmed. My boundaries were flimsy, and my money mindset was poor (literally). I wasn't living, I was surviving. I knew with every ounce of my being that I was not aligned with what I was doing. Was I good at it? Definitely. Was I happy? Absolutely not. I decided things needed to change. I diversified my business offerings to provide support for small businesses and entrepreneurs with business development while I figured out what I wanted to with my middle-aged self.

When I decide I want to do something, I am unstoppable. A fire is lit in my belly like a dynamite fuse. My instincts (with a dash of ADHD hyperfocus) drive me to achieve what I want to. One of my first clients came in the form of a marketing agency. They were attracted to my positivity, my ability to build real connections, and my ability engage people (an essential skill as a singer!). My work with them cemented my decision; I knew I needed to develop my branding and digital marketing skills, so I made my decision and I ploughed ahead. Within months I was committed to an apprenticeship and my goal was set: freedom to work on my own terms with people aligned to my values, energy, and creativity. People genuinely thought I was insane. I trusted that whatever transformation lay ahead was safe and I would grow into something better, just as those deciduous trees do, year after year. Change is safe.

I grew up in a working-class home in Northern England in the 1980s. My dad was a HGV driver and, from the early 1990s, my mum worked as a cleaner. They were both grafters. Hard work is all they had ever known. They worked hard so their children didn't have to go without as they had. We didn't have much money, but we knew no different. Home was often chaotic. Arguments and struggle were the mainstay. My parents' relationship was fractious, and they almost parted ways when I was a toddler. They both favoured the "devil they knew" and, inevitably, we all paid the price of their enduring yet misplaced loyalty and fear of change.

I was a gifted child. Not quite at the telekinesis-level of Matilda (I have no cool powers) but I had the most amazing memory and seemed to learn by osmosis. I coasted through school and never had to apply myself or revise. I wanted to be a hairdresser, but my mum would not allow it. She had *bigger plans;* as with many working-class parents, she wanted her children to *do better.* Mum did not want me to be a hairdresser, she saw it as *manual work for a pittance.* She didn't see the potential or value of being a business owner with her own salon(s), she just saw a ceiling of limited earnings and it didn't match *her* dreams for me. She favoured what she perceived to be safe and secure: a career in Law. Same again with the idea of me studying music and performing arts, even as a gifted singer. Hell, even as an established professional singer, my mum would accuse me of not being a *proper mum* to my children and say I was only *playing,* and it wasn't *a real job.* I genuinely believe that working-class people are conditioned to believe that work is hard, struggle is normal, and you should not find any enjoyment in what you do. I was determined to break this cycle of limited earnings and the oppression of aspirations and ambition.

My mum loved her family vehemently, but she wasn't readily able to see potential and possibility. She was a creature of habit. To her, predictability was safe. I, on the other hand, was a temptress of change and we invariably clashed. I didn't really know what I wanted to do with my life (I suspect many 18-year-olds don't) and I loved learning about English language and literature. My mum thought I should be doing Law. So, I submitted, and switched from studying English to Law. It always felt like I was living someone else's dream. I got a job as a paralegal shortly after graduating. I never pushed myself to be better or more. I loved Family Law and enjoyed working in this area of Law until I went into business on my own in 2021. I created my own glass ceiling to keep myself safe and without any real challenges to face. I wasn't happy and it never felt aligned.

My mum struggled with her mental health throughout her life. In my twenties, things between us became destructive. I had to move out of her house the night before my first Law degree exam as she leapt to attack me with scissors. This was not an isolated incident. My mum was like two different people rolled into one; one was the most beautiful soul; the other was the most tortured. Things became intense and, frankly, dangerous. In those earlier days, our relationship was complicated and symbiotic, with my mum seeing me as an extension of herself. She was not well, and it was having a huge impact on me. I was plagued with my own mental health battles until she finally got help in 2012 when she was diagnosed with and treated for schizophrenia. It felt like a monumental weight had been lifted – and I got my mum back, the most beautiful soul.

I have built a Kevlar-like resilience when it comes to change. I have survived every change, trauma, and difficulty I have endured. I would sooner try and fail than not try and be plagued with "what ifs." Change always allows room for growth and opportunity.

There was one thing I did fear though. In recent times, I had come to dread the day I would lose my mum and it felt like it was gaining momentum and catching up with me. It would often plague my thoughts like a devilish imp threatening to tear away my foundation. The taunts came thick and fast as my own family grew to love and cherish her, too. She was our heart, our home, our constant and our comfort. She was my best friend. We did everything we could together.

On the eve of Bonfire Night 2024, I lost my warrior mum. There is something indescribably agonising about losing your mum. You can never fully appreciate the impact and sheer devastation when you lose that person who underpinned your entire existence – until it happens. It's a finality you neither fully expect nor want, but a reality we must all endure at some time or other. I am eternally grateful for having had someone whose loss has created such a seismic impact on my existence, and I appreciate that is not everyone's reality. It was surreal seeing other people carrying on as though nothing had changed when my world was falling down around me. Life had inverted and moved in slow motion. This was not a change I found safe. I felt desperately alone and broken. But like the young trees in the wintertime, I'll learn how to bend (that may be a lyric from a Carpenters' song). I will learn how to bend because I have to. I have to accept that all change is normal and remind myself it is safe. Things will get better.

As with the trees in autumn, I have faith that better times lie ahead. I will come back from this with greater depth, unfettered resilience, and a renewed passion for life. I too will reclaim my power and once again be able to provide *nourishing knowledge* for others, and I will bloom better and stronger than before.

Losing my mum made me realise life has no guarantees but I cannot live in fear of that. Change is normal. Grief is normal. But there I was, still working to make other people richer and helping them to achieve their dreams, while keeping my own dreams at bay. My perspective has shifted. I now feel compelled to explore the possibility of setting up a business of my own. I want full creative autonomy, I want a strategy which matches my own values as well as eliciting business growth, and I want my work to make a difference to others.

I have always felt destined for greater things. I used to believe I was a *chronic underachiever,* but this removed my power; my path may have been meandering but the experiences and lessons I have learned along the way have gifted me an illustrious, diverse, and multifaceted skillset. I am highly skilled in a lot of areas, quick to learn and fast to adapt. I am energised and propelled by the many skills and the qualities I bring to the metaphorical table. I am not comfortable with the notion of settling or just accepting my lot. You see, success to me isn't determined by academic prowess, a big house in the country or a yacht on the Med. Success to me has evolved over time as I have fostered a greater level of consciousness and self-awareness. I have survived bleak times. *Every* time I have emerged stronger and wiser. Each time has brought me a step closer to understanding my purpose and my meandering path to true success. To me, true success is a balanced home and work life, a career in something that supports a critical flow of positive energy between myself and my clients, and the freedom to choose when and how I earn money. I value happiness, experiences, seeing the world, maintaining a sense of self beyond being a mother. There is more to me.

By the close of November 2024, I had set up my new business and branding, *Totally You Creative*. I have intentionally developed my brand with a strong emphasis on authenticity and the value of *real*. I help other women in business identify their purpose and to strategise their own brand and marketing to get them in front of the right audiences: people aligned to their values and aligned with their energy. People love learning about people and being YOU is the one thing no one else can mimic. Marketing isn't a *one-size fits all*. Different people (including you and your clients) value different things. We can only feel drawn to brands that provide solutions in a way that also aligns with our needs and values. You don't have to squeeze yourself into branding or marketing concepts that feel uncomfortable – unbutton those *branding pants* and let it all hang out! It is easier to be courageous and make changes if you have some faith in yourself (and if your pants are not restrictive) – trust that you know how to overcome challenges and focus on your end goal.

The ending of 2024 was not on my vision board. It certainly isn't a change I would have ever wanted to happen. I'd give anything to go back and love my mum a little more fiercely. The reality is I can't. That opportunity has gone. Opportunity does not wait for you.

Kim's Business Gold

I know I have so much to give and can help so many women to raise their visibility in their businesses. I have the strength. I am fearless. I trust my own worth and know I am resilient, determined, and strong enough to weather any storms. I understand that my value is determined by the spaces I move in; this has been fundamental in my decision to set up my own branding and marketing consultancy. I am aware of the qualities I am imbued with and the joy and connection I create with others. I want to be in the room where it happens (if you know, you know), networking with other women, learning and growing together, and supporting each other along the way. I want to help women to quash the negative self-talk and to stop talking themselves out of opportunities and potential.

Don't have the skills? Work out what you need to do to level-up. Don't have the connections? Start building your network now – your vibe really does attract your tribe. Get to know people and be genuinely interested in them. If you cannot bear the thought of having to attend in-person events, look at other options like online events or even groups on social media. Try to put your blinkers on to avoid *comparisonitis* and stay in your lane – you know which path you need to be on. People who feel drawn to your energy, purpose and value will trust you to accompany and support them on their own journeys. Curate your circle and cultivate your own happiness. Understand and be grateful for your journey – cherish your loved ones and do not forsake them or take them for granted. Don't delude yourself into believing people or opportunities will always be there – live in the now. Life is precious, even on the darker days. There is nothing selfish about pursuing happiness – you do not need to think, live and be small. If you know you are capable of more than you are currently achieving, allow yourself to explore and work out who you are and what will bring you happiness. Safe doesn't mean success but success is safe.

Just like the trees in spring, even when life has stripped you to your core, you will reclaim your power and once again provide sustenance for others with a renewed strength and a burgeoning sense of purpose. Enjoy the adventure and trust that you are safe. I give you permission to make the changes you want to make. Give yourself permission, too. What are you waiting for?

POWERHOUSE

Louise Cadman

About the Author

Louise Cadman is a Family Law Solicitor and Mediator who helps people going through divorce and separation to make the process quicker, cheaper, and less stressful.

Louise aims to help those going through this difficult chapter to step into their new chapter.

Having been a Family Law Solicitor for twenty years and seeing the cost and toll that the court system imposed on people, Louise moved into mediation to make it easier for the clients.

Louise helps families with children to make their own decisions in relation to what is best for their children, rather than putting it in the hands of the court, where a total stranger would tell parents what to do. Being a parent herself, Louise believes parents know their children better than anyone and are better equipped to decide what is best for them.

Louise also felt that parties often spent thousands of pounds arguing over their finances and how they were to be divided, often spending more money than was even in dispute.

After deciding that there had to be a better way for her clients Louise found that mediation was the perfect solution to help both parties come together and reach an agreement.

Louise has recently become an Accredited Family Law Mediator recognising her excellence in this area and commitment to helping people. She has an office in the Wigan area but also offers Zoom appointments, so can assist people all over the country, and she has even had clients as far afield as America that she has been able to assist reach agreement online.

Louise juggles work with her raising her family who keep her busy. In her spare time, Louise likes to spend time with her family, friends, and children, and has a passion for travelling with her family and visiting new places.

Louise is always happy to have a chat over the telephone if anybody wants any further information about Mediation.

Email: Advice@mediationtogether.co.uk

Website: www.mediationtogether.co.uk

Telephone: 07787114256

She Believed She Could, and She Did

Summer 2024, I am forty-four years old, and I am standing in the buzz and electricity of Times Square, New York with my girls and I have done it. I have achieved the vision I've had since the birth of my eldest daughter. Shopping in New York for her eighteenth birthday. I have never felt happier. So many times, in my life I didn't believe that I could do it, but here I am, eighteen years since I became a mum and in the same year we did London, Paris and New York. I am financially independent. I paid for it all for my girls, when just four years ago I was a shadow of myself and felt this was more out of reach than ever. You see for so long negative beliefs about myself held me back and this could have stopped me.

I still vividly remember aged eleven standing outside my form room at high school, being told I looked 'fat' by a boy. His voice still lives with me. I can still feel how I did in that moment. I wanted to cry. But I couldn't. You see, we remember and focus on the negative comments we hear in life, and those negative comments often determine who we become as a person and the confidence with which we live our lives. I couldn't cry and never have since in front of someone. This and other negative comments stayed with me, yet I now know that we can still achieve even if we don't fully believe.

From then on, I struggled to take compliments, and this formed limiting beliefs. At each step of my journey to qualifying to be a solicitor I believed that I was not good enough. In fact, it was never something I wanted to do, but I was a good girl and followed each next step. I did everything the right way – uni, good job, boyfriend, house, engaged, married and baby… but having it all in the right order meant nothing and I was divorced at thirty still consumed with negative beliefs. I have had it all and lost it all in many ways and finally in 2020 I did something for ME.

I launched my own successful business 'Mediation Together' as a qualified and accredited Family Law Mediator. If I hadn't made that change, then I would never have been able to take my girls to New York. Finally, I believed that I could… and I did. Since then, I have helped hundreds going through divorce and separation making the process easier, quicker, and cheaper.

I started my career as a solicitor having never known what I wanted to be. I grew up wanting to be an air hostess but at that time rules were stricter, and I wasn't good enough. I wasn't tall enough and I had contact lenses so did not meet the criteria. This left me feeling really deflated that I wasn't good enough to do the one thing I wanted to do.

I drifted from one step to the next, from high school to college, college to university, and university to the solicitor's training course. During my time as a trainee, I had a difficult time with a solicitor who appeared to be on a mission to destroy every ounce of self-worth and confidence I had, and virtually succeeded. I was miserable and would cry every morning getting ready for work, worrying I was going to mess up something and get shouted at and made to feel worthless. I had become like a hamster on a wheel, and I could not get off it. I was a nervous wreck and unable to think straight and making silly mistakes as I was so paranoid, I would physically shake at 3:30pm taking my post into my boss, who was supposed to be my mentor, to be signed.

Another negative memory that has lived with me was when I missed a typo on page fourteen of a twenty-page document. It said 'ion' instead of 'in.' I was shouted at for half an hour. This put me into freeze as I didn't retaliate. My freeze response was again to not cry but this resulted in being goaded to cry, being told, "You're deadpan," which has again lived with me as a limiting belief.

I did react, but in the privacy of the toilets. I broke down crying, which had become somewhat of a regular occurrence. I didn't feel good enough to be a solicitor; I felt like the worse trainee solicitor ever. I couldn't do anything right. I worried whether I would even qualify. I couldn't even spell, never mind be a solicitor.

I fought through the tears and meltdowns and qualified as a solicitor, but deep down I felt that I had cheated the system somehow. I wasn't good enough to be a solicitor and run my own cases.

Once qualified I enjoyed the job and bad memories faded, but, under the surface, they took root ready to appear every now and then to remind me I wasn't good enough.

Being a Family Law solicitor meant helping people and supporting them at the height of their emotions when going through some of the worst times in their life. People were happy with my service; what I achieved for them was working. I felt that I knew what I was doing, my clients were happy, no complaints, I was making money for the firm, and I felt that I knew what I was doing, and I was good at it. I had the job, the big house and car, the husband, and next on my list was children.

After having my first child, I realised my favourite thing to do was to be a mum and spend time with my child, but being a solicitor in what was still a man's world meant that I struggled to have a career and be the mum I wanted to be. I wanted to be the mum at school assemblies, I wanted to sit and eat tea together and ask my daughter about her day and put her to bed. I couldn't do that and work the hours that my career demanded of me.

Working 9-5, the juggle meant that once my daughter was in bed my working day started again and I would work till late into the night. Divorce followed when my daughter was two. My life had become about being a mum and work, I had no time for anything or anyone else. I had to be around for my daughter as much as possible and when I wasn't I had to work. I was again on that hamster wheel trying to prove I was good enough. I was trying to prove my worth as a working mum.

Pregnancy with my second child came and this further cemented my feeling that my role was to be a mum. I returned from pregnancy to a demotion from head of my department due to being part-time and having been on maternity leave. My confidence fell and that familiar feeling of not being good enough crept back in. This proved I couldn't have a career and be a hands-on mum. Old memories began to resurface of feeling not good enough, that I wasn't capable, that I wasn't good enough, I had failed.

March 2020 changed the lives of many people for all different reasons. By this time, I had moved in with my partner in a rented house and started working for him in his Family Law firm. By then the children were both at school but I still needed to be free to undertake all the childcare and school runs.

During lockdown we spent hours in the garden. The children played and made the best of the situation, doing schoolwork and enjoying the time that they had together away from their usual busy lives with school and activities such as dancing, which all went on Zoom. We had family meals, played games, and did family quizzes online with extended family and those memories are some of my best times when I allow myself to think of lockdown. Lockdown also brought about some of my darkest and worst times for reasons that are not for this book, and I choose to block lockdown out from my mind where possible, like it didn't really happen.

It was as we came out of lockdown and normality started to resume that I realised I did not know who Louise was anymore. I didn't know what was normal for me anymore, who I was, what I wanted or if what I felt or wanted even mattered. I had no real career anymore, I was no longer earning my own money, I had stopped wearing make-up and my clothes had taken a downturn. Some days I didn't even get dressed properly. I didn't know who I was anymore. I had changed from the girl who never went anywhere without high heels and poker straight hair, to someone living in flats and joggers and my hair, well that was making its own decisions.

I was getting what my partner paid me for working for him, but it wasn't the same. It didn't feel like my money was what I had earned. I felt totally financially dependent with no financial independence at all. A far cry from where I had been before I had children. I looked around and realised we were living in a rented house that we could get notice on at any time. I had gone from having a career as a solicitor with talk of partnership, living in my own house and driving my own car to nothing that was my own. Not only did I have no stability and security, but I realised my children didn't either. I had lost myself and I realised I was the only one who could find me again. Family and friends noticed I had changed. I knew that I had but I didn't know what to do about it and how to change back, that seemed impossible.

After the knock-on effect of lockdown, I was also starting to feel the toll of days arguing in court, fighting battles that I didn't always agree with, clients being unhappy because they didn't get the result they wanted. There are no winners and losers in Family Law, more often than not the judge would make a decision neither party was happy with. There were no good days, just days that were better than others. I never felt the system worked; there were so many flaws. The court system was backlogged. Cases were taking four months just to get a first hearing date and twelve to eighteen months to conclude. Emotions would run high, and clients would become frustrated and agitated. Their families' lives depended on these outcomes, children's futures, their relationships with their parents, families' abilities to rehouse themselves. It no longer felt that I was helping people. I felt there had to be a better way.

The pivotal moment came when I decided to take control, to retrain to give myself financial independence and the power and control over my own work life balance. I realised that I couldn't rely on others to make me happy and with that in mind I decided I had to make the changes and find who I was again. I had never dreamt of running my own business or being self-employed. Not for one minute did I ever feel I was good enough to do my job, never mind setting up my own business and people trust me to help them through their most difficult days, but needing security for my children pushed me on.

I had always fancied the idea of being a Family Law Mediator, but three weeks in London when I had two children felt impossible. Lockdown, however, brought about a new opportunity. I was able to train to be a mediator online as the world began to embrace Zoom opportunities.

I didn't know how I was going to make it work and was filled with self-doubt. I worried no one would send me any work, I wouldn't make any money, and ultimately that I wasn't good enough and I would fail.

"She believed she could, and she did," was a common phrase for my daughters growing up. Before exams I would make sure they had their bracelet that told them this and made sure I reinforced that message to them so felt it was time to practise what I preached. This became our family motto.

I was caring, I was a good listener, I was the friend that would be there for anyone, I would do anything to help anyone, surely, I was the perfect mediator. To listen to people and try to help them navigate the most difficult times of their life and make it easier, quicker, and cheaper for them was something I felt passionate about.

So, I started to believe that that I could. What if I was good enough and I could succeed? I had no excuse not to go for it... my partner was giving me money every month and I had already lost my career, my drive, my sense of self-worth and independence, so I really had nothing to lose!

I had spent years arguing in court, fighting fights I didn't believe in. Telling people what was best for their children, listening to judges tell parents who would have their child on what night for tea, who would take them to school, who would put them to bed.

I had children myself and realised that no one knows what's better for them than their parents. I could not imagine someone telling me what was best for my children. I did the course and after my first mediation session I knew this was what I was meant to do. I qualified as a mediator, and I decided to go it alone and set up my own business and be fully independent.

When my daughters were little, if I was out and my eldest was with my mum, it helped her to speak to me and hear my voice. With my youngest, speaking to me upset her so it was better not to speak to her. A perfect example of two children being different and knowing them and being their parent making decisions that met their individual needs. A judge doesn't know your child and what is best for them. I quickly developed the mantra, "no one knows what's better for your child than you." This is my most used line to clients, but also no one knows you or what's best for you other than you and in that what you are capable of. Don't let anyone tell you who you are, what you can do or what you can be! When we learn who we are and don't let anyone else tell us who we are is when we learn what we are capable of.

Through moving into mediation, I have not only created my own business and financial stability, but I know that I am helping so many people. Mediation can sometimes be overlooked within the system, with well-meaning relatives urging people to go to court, when in fact mediation can help in so many ways. It is generally quicker, cheaper, and much less stressful.

Louise's Business Gold

Mediation can improve communication between parties making it more amicable. It can be much more flexible as you do not need to wait for court timescales and importantly you are in control of the process, you get to choose the timescales and pick the days and times rather than the court choosing them for you.

Waiting for family court puts your life on hold, leaves you in a state of anticipation and fear and so mediation can make the process left invasive and stressful.

My clients have such positive outcomes and there is a high success rate where both parties are willing to mediate which is key to the success.

As I said, "no one knows what's better for your child than you." And my mission is to help people to be able to advocate for their children in the least stressful way. I seek to encourage parents to make the decisions themselves about their children and the time they spend with each parent rather than letting a stranger decide who doesn't know them, what they like, their favourite toy, book, teddy, their little ways, and routines.

All children are different and my two have very different outlooks and belief in themselves.

My younger daughter recently said she wanted to be King's Counsel. Only the top barristers in the county make King's Counsel, but her attitude is, 'someone has to, so why shouldn't it be me?' She believes she can do it and if that is what she wants to do she absolutely will.

This is so true in everything in life, someone has to be the one to do it. My elder daughter wouldn't try out for the university netball team, fearing she wasn't good enough. She scored more shots than the shooter of the university first team. She then realised that she had always been good enough but not believing in herself held her back. She was then asked to try out for the trampolining team and having realised she was better than she believed at netball she gave it a try and she made the team.

When I think back to my younger self and holding onto the negative voices and messages, I can see how they have held me back. Four years ago, I had lost myself and was almost swallowed up. I also loved being a solicitor and Family Law, but by following the mantra that I put in place for my girls I was able to help myself. I found my own belief and even though those negative voices still appear, I am able to still show up and back myself and in doing so help so many other families.

"She believed she could, and she did."

POWERHOUSE

Lucy Anjuna

About the Author

Lucy Anjuna is an online body transformation specialist and nutrition educator who founded an award-winning service, which has supported and inspired hundreds of women across the globe to regain control of their lives through health and fitness.

Prior to starting her company, Lucy worked for over fifteen years in various marketing and PR roles, providing clients with a wide range of services, from copywriting and campaign management to media relations and crisis communication.

Alongside her office job, Lucy's passion for helping others was channelled through her love for fitness and nutrition. Her business was born through a desire to bust the fitness and food industry myths to enable more women to make smarter choices so they can avoid ill health, gain confidence, and add years to their lives.

Lucy is a mum of two and has used her own experiences as a working parent to create a unique programme to guide her customers through the key pillars of success when it comes to achieving long-term fat loss and fitness results alongside a busy lifestyle.

Lucy is an avid weightlifter, lover of Sunday roast dinners, country walks, and old-fashioned movies and books.

Lucy's Elevate Body Transformation programme offers one-to-one coaching to UK and international customers. To apply, please contact Lucy via:

Email: info@lucyanjuna.com

Website: www.lucyanjuna.com

Social media: www.instagram.com/lucy_bodycoach

Always Be the Leading Lady in Your Own Life!

It's Monday – my favourite day of the working week. I've just got back from being interviewed for a Netflix documentary about my experience of becoming a successful female fitness entrepreneur. Earlier today, my four-year-old and I enjoyed a slow walk in the park after I decided last-minute to keep him off nursery. Why? Because I can. Because I've built the life I want to live; not the life someone else wants me to live.

Okay, so not every day is as glamorous as today but it's a real example of the opportunities and freedom I've created for myself through sheer hard work, grit, and determination.

The fact I can enjoy the luxury of being a mum and business owner on my own terms is a dramatic change to where I was just a couple of years ago. I used to despise Mondays and would spend most Sunday evenings on the sofa, dreading going into work; now I love them because I get to be an advocate for other women who want to be able to make smarter choices when it comes to their health and fitness, enabling them to positively transform across all areas of their lives.

As a mother of two young children, I now lead an award-winning online body transformation community, inspiring women across the globe to ditch fad diets and overcome fitness industry misinformation in favour of making smarter, everyday choices with their lifestyle to add years to their lives!

I'm here to tell you it's possible to completely transform yourself from being a stressed-out single parent in a dull, corporate job to becoming a CEO who enjoys financial freedom and the confidence to live life on your own terms.

I found success through some of the darkest and most challenging times of my life. Through twists and turns, I've discovered my own unique ability to empower other females to also live by the motto I use in life and business, which is, in the famous words of Audrey Hepburn, to 'Always be the leading lady in your own life.'

I love this saying because, once upon a time, I felt paralysed by caring too much about what others think, which negatively impacted my decision-making in areas of my life, such as my career and romantic relationships.

Thankfully, I released myself from the shackles in my mind and have realised the power of living authentically in line with my own wants and needs, and not by other people's standards.

The multiple side-hustles

I've always had a distinct thirst for learning new skills to make money on top of my day job.

By age twenty-one, I'd graduated from university with a PR and marketing degree. Alongside my then press office job, I began to attend evening classes to further my qualifications in other trades, enabling me to set up multiple part-time businesses in the health and beauty industries.

Although these businesses didn't necessarily use my best talents to set the world on fire, they served a purpose. They allowed me to feel in control of my own finances and decision-making, and I loved the empowering feeling of being my own boss and not having to follow someone else's rules.

Despite having a few side-hustles, I didn't understand how I could elevate any of my businesses to the next level and so didn't invest the time and effort required to do so.

I was working so excessively, in and around the corporate job, the enjoyment of being my own boss began to fade.

In 2022, things started to change. I decided it was time to stop juggling so many balls and focus on the one business that brought me joy; my personal training and fitness business, which I founded in 2016.

My love for teaching people about the power of nutrition and exercise became a talent, as did helping other women to have more self-belief.

By this point, I had already served hundreds of happy customers who told me they looked and felt the best they've ever felt because of my coaching and support. I desperately wanted to help more women but trying to manage additional customers and run a business alongside another full-time job was hard. It became even harder after becoming a mum.

Breaking free from the mould

Following yet another sixteen-hour day, I was sat in bed at midnight, working on my laptop, my toddler fast asleep next to me. I'd started my day at 7:30am and I was exhausted.

After experiencing a relationship breakdown, I became a single mum, juggling a full-time marketing management role and a part-time personal training business. Every day felt like a never-ending 'to-do' list of life admin and work tasks.

On top of trying to keep afloat financially, I was struggling to accept my father's terminal cancer diagnosis. The pressure of trying to balance work, be a mother and care for my family was intense. I felt like an elastic band that was about to snap.

After eleven years, I found myself in a monotonous, corporate marketing management role and I felt tired and uninspired. I felt a yearning to break free from societal norms. Surely there was more to life than just working for someone else, sleeping, eating, and repeating?

I had a massive itch I wanted to scratch. Growing up, I ditched the idea of moving to London to enrol in drama school because my parents, although supportive of my creative talents, encouraged me to get a university degree in a 'safer' profession. I did what I felt family and society expected me to do.

My day job was well-paid and safe, but it felt uninspiring, and I was starting to resent it.

With evenings and weekends taken up with serving customers, my personal training job was ticking along nicely, and it gave me enough additional income towards household bills and childcare (this was important as I wasn't in receipt of any benefits or other financial support).

I was a self-employed personal trainer in a back-street gym in Blackpool, with a mixture of in-person and online customers. I was in a dilemma. I adored helping people to transform their lives through the work I did in my business – but I couldn't invest enough resources for it to become my main source of income. I was tired and the very work that brought me a huge sense of passion and pride was also the very thing that was exhausting me.

I'd come home from my day job, and I'd be on the laptop again as soon as I'd put my son to bed, often working until the early hours of the following morning to ensure customers were being served. I became resentful towards work and withdrawn.

Life is too short to play it safe

Then the bomb dropped.

My beloved dad reached the end of his desperate five-year fight for survival. The protector of the family was gone, leaving my mum, his wife of forty years, and my brother and I, completely devastated.

With the world as I knew it completely upside down, I fell into a depression.

After several months of not feeling the same motivation towards business or life, one day I had a moment of clarity. I was sat looking at old photos of dad, and the television turned itself on to a programme called, 'Never Give In.' My dad never gave up on anything he put his mind to, and I knew it was my duty to continue his legacy and do the same.

And literally, just like that, I woke up the following day with a new sense of determination. From that point onwards, I knew what I had to do – I needed to quit the day job, become a full-time boss, apply for a mortgage, and start becoming the leading lady in my own life!

The mortgage dilemma

The next life goal I was working towards was securing a mortgage on a home for my son and I, but I needed my employment pay slips as proof of income. This meant prolonging my employment, which was counterproductive towards my goal of becoming a full-time boss.

I decided if I was to catapult my online body transformation service into a better financial position and quit the office job sooner, I needed to enlist some specialist help.

I employed a business mentor. Not one of these 'pop-up' social media people who claim to help you become a six-figure business overnight, but someone who had a proven track record of success within my industry and who cared about supporting coaches, not only in becoming better entrepreneurs but also better coaches.

It was a huge gamble and a bold move. I decided to take several thousand pounds from my house deposit fund and go all in with the business mentoring.

I figured if other health and fitness professionals with less experience or qualifications than I had were able to generate a greater income, there must be something I was missing.

Within twelve months, the investment into my mentor paid off. I'll never forget the day I received the call from my financial advisor with the exciting news. Even though the country was heading into a recession, I'd positioned my business enough for the bank to approve my mortgage application. I cried so many happy tears. As a thirty-eight-year-old, single mum, I was finally living life on my own terms and, despite the country heading into a recession, I was free to resign from my office job.

I quit

In all honesty, I suck at being an employee in an office. I'm too much of a rule-breaker and my life works much better when I'm not following someone else's script.

In 2022, six years after starting what was originally a side hustle, I finally found my courage to leave a job I began to despise. I began to embrace the adventure of being a full-time entrepreneur, while navigating single parenthood in my thirties.

This was the dramatic turning point for me in business. Within the first twelve months of becoming a full-time CEO, I was able to serve more customers, earning more than twice as much as my corporate job, and was able to structure my working week in a way that helped me be more present as a mum (massive win!).

Lucy's Business Gold

Top Body Transformation Tips

Ditch the all or nothing attitude. Instead, integrate smarter decision-making into your daily routine, without the pressure to be perfect all the time. We don't always want to avoid cake and wine, and why should we?

Be patient. Slow down; it's not a race. If you're on a fat loss journey, losing an average of a pound each week is far more sustainable than losing several pounds all at once and then piling the fat back on later down the line.

Know your why. Having a clear reason for living a healthier lifestyle will help you stay consistent. For example, do you want to be a great role model for your children? Or is it to become more confident? Your purpose should be support for all the things you want outside of the gym or eating well.

Focus on building muscle. Women who want to be more toned, lose body fat and fit their clothes better, should focus more on resistance training (for example, using weights).

Consume consciously. We have access to so much useful information about the foods we eat on social media and the internet but, sadly, there's a lot of misinformation out there, too.

Choose your pain. Getting fit can be painful but it's not as painful as living with ill health. By taking better care of yourself, you can avoid most diseases and add years to your life!

Have a plan. Invest in your health and hire a coach. Of course, this is the best advice I can give to any female CEO who seems to struggle to get in shape and keep the results. We're quick to inject cash into our business and we should treat our bodies with the same respect. If you have a plan to follow for your workouts and diet, you're more likely to succeed.

Tips on Creating More Freedom Within Business

Work when you need to work. Building a successful business isn't easy. The luxury of freedom to design your own time only comes with hard work. There were days when I cried through sheer exhaustion (and still do from time to time!) to get my business thriving. However, you get out what you put in.

Stop over-analysing. Make decisions and use a trial-and-error approach. Procrastination or overthinking the data used to be one of my downfalls. I now realise it was due to a fear of failure and not achieving perfect results. It's better to trial new tactics in business and refine them later, than never to have tried at all.

Block out the noise. I've learned to be aware of the competition but not allow other people's businesses to distract me from my own mission. Originality is key.

Follow carefully. Take advice from others but only from those who are where you want to be. I chose to invest in a top business mentor because I knew of his success in my industry.

Network. Get used to collaborating with others and network as much as possible. Simply meeting up with fellow business owners has generated thousands of pounds of income for me this year alone.

Daily routine. I don't get up at 5am to meditate or take ice baths; I create a daily power-list and I prioritise my work tasks. I also ensure I schedule in some form of fun or down-time into my week. That could be as simple as making time for a bath with Jazz FM playing in the background! I do this to avoid the all-or-nothing approach (I like to practise what I preach!).

POWERHOUSE

Caroline Hargreaves

About the Author

Caroline Hargreaves is a ICF & CPD certified somatic trauma informed coach and narcissistic abuse specialist, trained in positive psychology, who empowers those seeking healing and growth so they can move forward and reach their true potential.

Caroline is a member of the School of Trauma Informed Positive Psychology, The Association for IEMT Practitioners and a founding Brand Partner with The Mental Wellbeing Company.

Caroline is committed to creating a ripple effect of healing and growth within families, organisations, and communities. She does this through coaching and delivering workshops both in person and online across the globe.

Caroline blends a unique range of techniques to meet each client's specific needs, including coaching, Brainspotting, IEMT, Reiki, and hypnotherapy, helping create lasting change through integrating somatic healing and nervous system regulation.

Before establishing her coaching business, Caroline gained nearly twenty years of experience in operations, change and project management in the public sector. Her desire to make a difference, combined with her lived experience and personal journey of healing from trauma and overcoming adversity, has shaped her passion for supporting others to embrace their full potential and break free from the struggles of the past.

Caroline enjoys creating memories with her three children and is dedicated to building a fulfilling life for her family. Together they love bringing Mindful Kids classes to Blackpool, bringing other caregivers and their children together nurturing mindfulness and emotional resilience in children.

Caroline is available for one-to-one coaching, group coaching, workshops, and collaborations.

Email: Caroline-Hargreaves@outlook.com

Website: linktr.ee/CarolineHargreaves

Social media:

www.linkedin.com/in/caroline-hargreaves-4450212a2

This is Not How My Story Ends

Sitting, at peace, in the local coffee shop writing – this is my happy place. I find myself smiling and chatting to others, latte in hand, allowing myself to enjoy a sweet treat without feeling guilty. This is my self-care and something that an old version of me would have struggled with. I felt so stuck in my life that even this moment felt so out of reach. For many years, surviving on coffee and cake was one of my trauma responses, but now, this is a safe place where I feel confident to be me and enjoy being me.

What might seem like a small change is in fact huge for me, as now I am unstuck from those old feelings, thoughts, and beliefs since I have created that change for myself.

But let me share a secret with you, trauma responses often show up for me. In fact, I was excited to collaborate in this book until hearing the title 'POWERHOUSE.' It threw me into panic, I wanted to run away and hide. I felt my heart racing, heat rising in my body, and that familiar ache in the pit of my stomach.

So, if you're reading this thinking you're not a Powerhouse or you sometimes find yourself stuck, crippled with self-doubt and fear that your life will never change, this chapter is for you.

You see, I believed a POWERHOUSE was an extrovert, a confident expert, making a difference, making waves in the world in powerful ways. I told myself whoever you think you are, it's not that, you're not a strong, focused Powerhouse of a woman. You can't do this!

I sat with it, the discomfort, fear, self-doubt, my inner critic, and all the other parts of me that showed up, welcoming them with curiosity and compassion and coming back to my true self realising I am a Powerhouse bringing my own unique POWER.

We're all unique, it's what makes us amazing and attracts people, energy, and business to us. It's not about fitting in or being liked by everyone; it's about finding our flow and showing up authentically and feeling safe to do that.

When we struggle with that, then it's time to create change.

For me, my soul mission is to create change for myself, my children, and as many others as I can. I hope my story inspires you to create lasting change.

My journey is one of breaking generational cycles, finding myself and the freedom to create a life and business where I thrive.

A journey of healing, growth, transformation, and resilience from overcoming trauma and abuse, becoming a solo parent, a life on the outside which appeared normal and happy but, on the inside it was a different story, it was a struggle.

Let's go back to my childhood, looking back I can see now that's where it began, where I learnt it wasn't 'safe' just being me and so growing up I lost my core self, my identity. I didn't know what I didn't know, it's only with self-awareness, healing and embracing post traumatic growth, seeing the world through a trauma-informed lens I now understand myself, my life, others, and the world so much better, with a new curiosity and compassion. I absolutely love this new me.

Born in 1983, a tiny 3lb 4oz, eleven weeks premature, hooked up to beeping machines alone and scared in my incubator. The world is a scary place when we come into it and if we lack connection with our caregivers (a basic human need) survival mode kicks in. I was a tiny baby primed for survival and that became how I lived my life until recent years. Looking back, I can see why I became an anxious co-dependent, relying on other people to complete my identity. I had a huge fear of rejection, putting others' needs first, often trauma-bonded in relationships, losing myself even more in the process and creating lots of survival adaptations to keep myself safe along the way.

By the age of three I had the belief I wasn't loveable, at five I wasn't good enough, by nine I wasn't important, by thirteen I wasn't worthy. I left home at nineteen and found myself even more lost in a string of toxic and unhealthy relationships. I thought this must be it, this must just be how life is for me.

I spent most of my life struggling with stress, anxiety, and depression; every few years sinking into depression, wiping me out for a couple of weeks, struggling to get through the day and not understanding why. Talking therapies helped a little, validating my feelings so then I'd brush myself off and carry on, until the next time.

Fast forward to a few years ago. I started a narcissistic abuse trauma recovery programme and I was stunned when I learnt we must be taught connection, co-regulation, and how to feel safe. A quote stood out for me from Dr Gabor Mate, "Children don't get traumatised because they get hurt, they get traumatised because they are alone with the hurt," and I felt that. It gave me goosebumps.

I'm from the generation where children were to be seen and not heard and behave how others wanted us to. A generation driven by fear and shame-based behaviours prioritising control and conformity at home, school, and in the workplace, a generation that suppressed emotions and who they were to please others and fit in.

I feel sad that although people are always doing their best in any given moment, so many of us were never taught to feel safe to be ourselves; yet we wonder why society struggles with their emotions and mental health. Imagine the difference in the world if we could create safe spaces free from shame and judgement, with an understanding of the importance of connection; the world hasn't changed yet – but I have, and it fills me with hope, autonomy, and freedom.

I started work at thirteen, not knowing what I wanted to do when I 'grew up.' It was confusing being told who I was and who I wasn't, how to behave. I spent years living my life for others, pleasing them whilst doubting myself and losing more of myself. I spent my life looking externally to fill a big dark, scary, and lonely hole in my soul, not knowing everything I needed was already within me, I'd just never been shown.

I got a good secure job, settled down and was supposed to live happily ever after... spoiler alert: that didn't happen.

In my late thirties I found myself having to rebuild my life, heading for divorce with three children under three, nearly bankrupt after a failed business venture, starting fresh in a new home, so far from what my life was supposed to be.

It was the hardest, messiest, and most challenging time. I was scared, lost and alone – definitely not a great place for an anxious, people pleasing, co-dependant. Somehow, I found the strength to get up each morning and function for the sake of the kids, but I was at rock bottom of survival mode. It became 'Groundhog Day,' counting down the hours until bedtime, looking forward to my childfree nights so I could go out partying and numb the pain.

Until one day something shifted within me, I was sitting in a haze watching my children play, overwhelmed with grief, anger, loss, and a huge amount of fear about the future. I was barely functioning, I existed, and suppressed so much. I had been stuck in a cycle for so long, repeating old patterns, getting through with emotional eating, drinking, spending money, keeping busy, to the other extreme where I had no energy to do anything, even getting dressed or taking a shower was a struggle. I started to hate myself, I had lost myself completely, it felt heavy and dark. I was tense with tight shoulders, a clenched jaw, always feeling on edge, a constant pressure in my chest, and like I was holding my breath. I was stuck in functional freeze.

I was disconnected from myself, the world and my children, struggling to find joy in being a parent, in anything and in that moment that realisation washed over me, tears streamed down my face, a bubbling anger about how my life wasn't, a deep sadness, my heart ached as I felt a warm rush of love not only for my children but for myself and in that moment I told myself, "Hell no, this is not how my story ends."

I finally admitted that my marriage was over. It was time to divorce and to accept I was on my own, but I could be okay on my own. It was time to embrace the difficult journey of navigating life as a solo parent, to create change, break cycles and generational patterns for the sake of my own health and so the children didn't grow up in a life where 'mummy wasn't happy.' It was time for me to heal, so I could grow and thrive.

I wanted more, I was destined for more, capable of more, there was hope and limitless possibilities if I chose to BE the change. Everyone has the power and potential to break free from what holds them back, to live their best life.

I was born to thrive, not only survive.

I was surviving on coffee and cake, afraid to be alone. I was emotional, anxious, scared, laughing off the surviving on coffee jokes parents make, but this ran a little deeper. Life was overwhelming and overshadowed by the fear of the unknown. I didn't know what would come in regard to our future, the divorce, child arrangements, but I was free and realised if I didn't do the inner work, I was going to stay stuck, full of fear, anger, lacking confidence, and not feeling safe to be me, repeating old patterns. I could numb the pain with drunken nights out, copious amounts of caffeine and lots of masking, but I decided enough was enough.

Many say your trauma makes you stronger. NO, it made me traumatised! It damaged me, gave me sleepless nights and complex PTSD, made me sensitive, insecure, emotional, and overwhelmed. It kept me in a state of hypervigilance, stuck in survival mode, feeling powerless, like I was falling apart inside. It made me build huge walls and disconnect.

I didn't need to be strong – I needed to feel safe. So, that's what I have done, by healing, dealing with stuff that wasn't my fault, taking my power back, creating a life I choose and value.

Completing the trauma recovery programme was a pivotal moment in my life; it was here I turned my pain into my power. I focused on the inner work and found meaning and purpose. In becoming unstuck I discovered my passion. I stepped into post traumatic growth; it's not always comfortable here as I heal and overcome my past experiences, learn about myself, and continue on my journey to create the life I want filled with joy, love, and abundance.

My younger self often shows up to protect me, I become frozen with fear often getting shutdown with a migraine to stop me in my tracks. My fear shows up as doom scrolling, comparing myself to others, everything to stop me stepping out of my comfort zone. The self-doubt creeps in, the fear of being vulnerable, visible, and telling my story just as it did when I was triggered by the word 'Powerhouse.' And do you know why? Because of the fear and pain of being judged, shamed, or disliked. This is my younger self asking, "What if I'm not good enough?" So, I will tell you what I told that younger part of me, "You are good enough, you were born good enough, and you deserve this."

I am worthy of this just as much as anyone else.

Fear held me back my whole life, fear had me struggling to say, "No," running away from healthy, secure relationships; fear stopped me showing up in my business. I lived a life consumed with feeling like a failure, broken, like there was something wrong with me, stuck; not feeling a good enough daughter, sister, girlfriend, wife, mum, friend, employee, businesswoman; feeling unworthy of love, time, money or taking up space.

When I learnt about trauma and being trauma-informed it changed the narrative from 'What is wrong with you?' to 'What has happened to you?' Dr Gabor Mate said, "Trauma is not what happens to you, it's what happens inside of you as a result of what happens to you."

Through healing what happens inside of me, learning to regulate my nervous system, rewire my brain and reconnect with myself, I found safety, compassion, and courage to rewrite my story. The nervous system is something I wish every person understood. In reconnecting with myself at a nervous system level my capacity to cope with challenges has increased, I found the strength to reclaim my power.

We can create calm and supportive environments through nervous system education and regulation; it's through that and the power of healing I began to fill that hole in my soul. It enhanced my mental health and wellbeing and helped me find balance both personally and professionally.

My journey brings me new experiences that test my nervous system capacity and flexibility, meaning lots of behaviours and emotions show up along the way:

- Procrastination.
- Inner critic.
- Self-sabotage.
- Anxiety.
- Overthinking.
- Anger.
- Dissociation.
- Emotional eating.
- Catastrophiser.

These are parts of my trauma response, remember it didn't feel safe to be me, so it's no wonder my power faded way. It's my body adapting to the environment to keep me safe, to survive based on my past experiences, remembering the pain my younger self felt when she came into this world, right through to my experiences today. My nervous system did an amazing job protecting that younger version of me, always working for me with a loving intention even if it had destructive consequences over the years. My body was perfectly happy staying stuck, it was safer to stay that way than to risk feeling the pain and humiliation my younger self had ever again.

I now thank my nervous system when it does this and I continuously work on myself, expanding my comfort zone, healing the wounds of my past and showing up in SELF energy. Now when I notice I am feeling activated, anxious, or triggered, I bring awareness to it, I use what's in my toolkit to overcome it. I love nervous system regulation and the changes it creates for myself, my children, and my clients.

Caroline's Business Gold

Let me share a few regulation tips with you.

- I invite you to take a moment to pause, notice your feet on the floor, notice what's around you, what you see, hear, smell, and feel. Ground yourself in the present moment and notice how that feels in your body.

- 5-2-8 breath – breath in for 5 – hold for 2 – exhale for 8 (repeat a few times until you feel calm).

- Butterfly hug – place your hand on your opposite shoulder then alternately tap one hand and then the other. You can also take slow deep breaths and say affirmations like, "I am safe," or "I am calm."

Find what works to bring you back to a place of calm and presence, maybe focusing on the breath, a butterfly hug, grounding yourself, getting out in nature, a soak in a bubble bath to rest and recharge, or perhaps dancing round the house to your favourite tunes to shake off that sympathetic energy.

Remember to pause, breathe, and check in with yourself regularly.

I am eternally grateful for my journey and how my experiences have shaped the person I am today and my ability to continue to heal, grow and thrive as Caroline, a parent and businesswoman.

Time is not a healer and healing is a journey, the work is never done and that's the beauty in it. Once I started to heal somatically, understanding physiology and the nervous system it was life changing!

It was another messy journey but of self-discovery, with lots of uncertainty, tears and holding my breath until I was ready to explore deeper, to hold space for myself, to heal my inner wounds from the past and to align with my true self and higher self to thrive.

I took it slowly, navigating through the discomfort, my nervous system liked our old ways, we had survived that far so it took time, awareness, and action to create change. Plus, when we do too much too soon it can shut us down even more, the nervous system becomes overwhelmed. I am continuously creating change with my coaching skills, breathwork, journalling, meditation, reiki, checking in with my nervous system, vagus nerve toning, getting out in nature and of course a visit to my favourite coffee shop.

I reclaimed my power when I forgave myself, it felt like a huge weight lifted, that hole in my soul wasn't as dark anymore when I released the shame I had been carrying for so long. It finally feels safe to be me and I want others to feel that too.

I transformed from surviving to thriving. I've found strengths in what I previously saw as weakness, I'm strong, passionate, empathetic, curious, resilient, insightful, and compassionate, that's what helps me to create change.

I've broken cycles and generational patterns, in healing myself I am healing my children, my grandchildren – in fact seven generations. I've given us the gift of a connection, with the skills to navigate life and the unshakeable belief that we will succeed.

I am creating transformational change, the kind my younger self could only dream of, she would be incredibly proud of what I am creating for her, for me, for my children and for others.

That moment when I decided it wasn't how my story ends it was the catalyst for change, where I became a change maker and a Powerhouse. My healing journey and choosing to create change brought me peace, empowerment and to a place where I now help others on their unique journey to live their best life too.

You can create change for yourself and become unstuck. Life doesn't have to be like this and remember this is not how your story ends either.

POWERHOUSE

Nicole Louise Geddes

About the Author

Nicole Louise Geddes is a professional performer turned multi-passionate entrepreneur. She is the founder of two successful businesses; PerformerPreneur, her business coaching service, confidence building framework and collaborative community, supporting performers and entrepreneurs to step into the spotlight and level up their finances, life, business, and self-belief; and her longstanding entertainment company, Manic Stage Productions, which has supplied acts and artists both nationally and internationally to events on land and at sea since 2005.

Sharing her showbiz secrets and business-building knowledge to help others show up, succeed, and feel safe to be seen, has fast become her biggest passion. She has been celebrated and featured on multiple business podcasts, stepped on international stages as a keynote speaker, appeared in the national press, and most recently crowned a finalist for an 'Inspirational Woman' award.

As the chapter alludes to, over the years Nicole has had many exciting opportunities unfold. From performing with Kylie Minogue, to choreographing shows in New York City and producing pop-up entertainment across the entire P&O cruise ship fleet. Stepping confidently into every new and exciting spotlight with ease is her thing. She even moved her whole family to live in Oman in 2023 for a two-year adventure to live out her dream of running her businesses in the sun.

Nicole invites you to step out of the shadows, start to build your confidence and evolve with her help. If you know you are ready to shine in the many spotlights of your life and reach new heights, then working with Nicole through one of her many professional services is most certainly the next exciting step to take.

Podcast:

podcasts.apple.com/gb/podcast/the-showbiz-side-hustle-podcast/id1758059348

Website: www.performerpreneur.co.uk

Social media: www.instagram.com/performerpreneur/

Show Up Like a Showgirl

I stand centre stage ready to deliver my keynote on confidence, 'Show Up Like a Showgirl.' My eight *stagey secrets* to confidently step into the spotlights of your life has been shared countless times both on and offline! But this time is different, this time is a 'pinch me' moment. I am on a stage, standing in a spotlight, unable to see the dark seats in front of me or the faces of those ready to hear me speak.

A familiar feeling moves through my body as I wait. The feeling is not fear, I am not met with a chorus of nerves or a deep feeling of dread. I do not want to bolt from the spotlight and exit stage left. In fact, as the bright stage lights shine down on me and cover my face and body in a warm golden glow, I am transported to a familiar place. I feel safe in the spotlight's warm embrace.

It's as if the theatre's lighting technician has dialed down, not only the auditorium lights, but the intensity and the insecurities others feel when navigating and showing up in the spotlights of their life. As the auditorium lights dim so does the negative voice inside my head. When the follow spot button is turned to on, my 'leading lady' switch is flicked and my professional performer instincts kick in. I can't lie, I feel alive as the eyes of the silent audience watch me and wait. The showgirl within me steps up and into action, I take a slow deep breath, stand tall and take up space. Lift my eyes, smile, and begin to calmly and confidently 'show off' what I have prepared, practised, and worked so hard to be able to stand here deliver and do.

Many of my clients have lost the courage to take centre stage. They admit they have spent years stood in the shadows of their own life, too afraid to stand tall and proud. They speak of feeling unsafe to be seen or heard, not confident enough to share their thoughts and opinions with the rest of the world. All unsure how they will succeed without the confidence they need.

Yet here I am doing the things they dream of with ease. It may be a different spotlight, but each time I step on stage I am grateful for my industry training and how it translates. Decades in the entertainment industry as a professional dancer, singer, and circus performer, still serve me so well. My years treading the boards on stage and screen are a lifetime ago, but the secrets of my showbiz career help me navigate the here and now effortlessly. I certainly don't take for granted the security I feel in the spotlights of my life. It truly saddens me to see so many wonderful people lack the confidence they need to show up and shine.

As a child I was full of energy, creativity, and enthusiasm, with an unapologetic confidence that would make a stage out of every room. Looking back, I don't remember a time when I wasn't dancing in the mirror or singing my heart out along with the Disney princess on the TV screen. Performing for my parents happened daily, making my little sister do acrobatics with me to the radio recorded songs from the 'Top 40.' How many of us can relate? Who remembers those younger years, when taking centre stage felt safe?

Being theatrical, stagey, dramatic, 'confident' was celebrated in my household growing up. I have clear and happy memories that it was safe to 'show off.' From a young age my performing arts skills were nurtured through dance classes, singing lessons and drama activities. I spent every hour I could performing for whoever would watch, and when they wouldn't, I'd line my teddy bears up and sing into my hairbrush. I guess to those close to me, it's no wonder I went on to pursue a professional performing career as a showgirl and circus artist. But how did this foundation of theatre build my confidence in the spotlight and support my pivot into becoming a successful business leader and entrepreneur?

What comes first the chicken or the egg? Does success follow confidence or does confidence lead to success?

I wonder if the encouragement and acceptance of my extroverted ways from my family and friends is the reason I thrived on and off the stage. Or was it always going to be that way? Was it written? Is confidence created, or do we have it from day one? It's no secret that external factors chip away at our confidence and create doubt. We have all experienced that. So why and how do some people succeed seemingly more easily? I have come to believe my performer background and industry resilience plays a big part in my success story. Having the ability to bat off the world's negativity, hold tightly on to the childlike skill to spin, dance and sing unapologetically. Being loud and proud without even saying a word, dulling down the feelings of self-doubt and continuing to prioritise nurturing my self-belief, I believe are all skills I acquired thanks to the highs and lows of my showbiz career.

It's fair to say my confidence was nurtured through a childhood full of positive experiences and opportunities to perform. For me, being in the spotlight was safe. I can very clearly remember being celebrated for 'being brave' to step on stage. Endlessly praised for my singing and dancing skills, loud voice, broad smile, and enthusiasm for taking part in performances, classes, and competitions. I remember the feeling I got from the applause, the feeling of acceptance as audience members clapped and cheered me on. On reflection this feeling was a regular occurrence for me. My life as a child revolved around the arts. I think applause and acceptance can truly nurture a deep-rooted self-belief that you are enough, and you deserve to succeed.

I can assure you not every scenario was a positive experience. I do recall a time when the cheerleading and unspoken permission to take up space did stop. On stage and in the studio, it remained steadfast and safe, but in public, in the 'real' world, I was, told to, "Sit down, shut up," and to, "Stop showing off!"

As I grew up, I heard the words, 'stop showing off' from the world far too often. In school it was best to sit back, wear black and do what was asked. Bossy girls were berated, loud girls were told to hush, and that's just the adults in the room. Add the complexities of puberty which unquestionably creates a confusion within us all, and you are suddenly dodging the bullying ways of the peers who are threatened by the few, who are still happy to be seen and show up in their own skin.

At what age and why were you told to "Stop showing off?" Did these words lead you to shy away from the spotlight and reside in the shadows of your own life? I would love to gift you the theatrical tools and techniques you need to take even a small step back into the light. I am so excited to share my *stagey secrets* with you. I hope the tips, tricks and hacks that follow will dull down your imposter syndrome and build your confidence to 'Show Up Like a Showgirl,' succeed unapologetically and 'show off' authentically.

Unsurprisingly, the negative messages towards being confident and being brave enough to take up space didn't stop at school. As I entered the entertainment industry professionally, it became apparent very quickly that not everyone wanted me to succeed. Finding where I was going to be supported, comfortable and encouraged in a sea of competition looked impossible. Luckily, I found a small group of peers who like me put collaboration over competition. We encouraged each other through auditions and life in the industry to stay true to ourselves and embrace our authenticity. My self-belief and confidence survived this tricky time thanks to the people I chose to surround myself with and it's a life lesson that hasn't left me.

Navigating adolescence through to adulthood is tough, fact. It's no surprise that positive experiences and positive connections with the right people can boost confidence and self-esteem. Yet it's sad that so many of us have a memory full of situations, comments, and events where we didn't feel safe to be seen. It's no wonder so many of us now shy away from the spotlights in our own life and let others take the lead and step centre stage.

The message that I want to share with you is that if somewhere along the line you lose your confidence it IS possible to find it again. Confidence is in fact a trait that can be learned. Yes, I promise you, you can learn how to be confident, develop it over time, surround yourself with cheerleaders and once again feel safe to shine.

Brian Tracy says, "Confidence is a habit that can be developed by acting as if you already have the confidence you desire to have."

Before I share with you the 'hacks' to help your confidence grow, I want to share with you first and foremost the gold. THE most important part of my 'Show Up Like a Showgirl' signature talk and framework is very much overlooked by the many others who try to teach confidence skills across any industry. In my expert opinion and experience, the biggest piece of the confidence puzzle and the most important business gold that I need you to know as you work on building your confidence to be seen and shine, is... community.

"To truly feel safe to show up, show off and succeed, you need the one thing many of us are missing; community."

Community is key!

If the spotlight is a circle, think of it as a circle of trust. You will only ever feel wholeheartedly safe to step into its bright light and place the spotlight on you and your life IF the spotlight is warm and welcoming. It's then and only then that you will step out of your own way, embrace your authenticity, turn to the voice inside your head that continues to creep in to keep you 'safe' and unapologetically say... "I am in the right circles, I am surrounded by support, cheerleaders, community, IT IS SAFE TO SHOW OFF."

Finding the people who light you up, cheer you on and celebrate your success is the most liberating place to be. I learned this without even realising it as a young child being praised and clapped on and off stage and again both through performing arts college and once I had found my 'best' pro performing friends in the industry. The theatre spotlight is a safe place for me. The audience are there ready and waiting for your performance to be a huge success. Every single person in the production company is there working together to support you and each other to succeed. From backstage, to front of house, production team, patrons, and performers, EVERYONE is part of the show's community, and that community support, encouragement, positive reinforcement, collaboration, and collective energy is the KEY.

Nicole's Business Gold

In addition to encouraging you to find your community, as promised, there are also entertainment industry secrets, hacks, and performer superpowers I want to share to help you 'Show Up Like a Showgirl' and swiftly feel more comfortable and confident in any spotlight. Remember, if confidence is a habit, then we know it's possible to use the three main components of habit formation: the context cue, behavioural repetition, and the reward, to turn your confidence around. You CAN take action, commit, and train yourself daily to feel safe to 'show off.'

Mindset

"If you believe you can, you will and if you believe you can't you are right." Turn the clock back and remember how it felt to believe you would grow up to be an astronaut, a pop star, a footballer or, for me, a professional performer. Rebuild this childlike presumption (and this time don't let the world tell you you can't), by building positive affirmations, daily gratitude, vision boards and manifestation into your daily routine. Start to see and believe the confident version of you exists. Become the person you aspire to be in your mind so that you feel comfortable and confident in the shoes and spotlights of your future self.

5 Ps

I would never have stepped on stage without taking class, attending rehearsals, having my ballet shoes on, or my hair in a bun and the same goes for life in any spotlight. "Proper preparation prevents poor performance." It is very rarely the lack of ability that scuppers a person's success. In whatever spotlight you pursue, make sure you prioritise preparation and planning. Confidence can and will grow with a commitment to becoming the person you want to be. Putting the 5 Ps to the top of your to-do list will make stepping into the spotlight more comfortable and when you are comfortable in any situation it is much easier to feel and be confident.

Practice

We have all heard the expression, 'Practice makes perfect,' but what about, 'Practice makes permanent?' For your confidence to become a fixed asset and valued trait you can rely on in any spotlight and situation, you must practise, practise, practise. Start with practising the art of 'looking' confident. As any showgirl will tell you it's the discipline in the studio that shines on stage. Practise the following performer hacks and see how they help to build a more permanent look of confidence in you.

Posture

Pull your shoulders back, throw your arms in the air and hold your head high. This typical performer stance will instantly tell your brain you are okay in the spotlight. It's so important to take up space, show up for yourself by standing tall, stop hiding and being small. Try it and see how instantly more confident you feel and are seen to be.

Breath

Breath control is so important when performing and you can use it to your advantage too. Trick your brain into believing you are not nervous, worried, or scared, by breathing deep into the diaphragm rather than shallowly in the upper chest. By dropping your breath down into your diaphragm, you will instantly feel more confident in the spotlight and situation, less alert and more in control.

Smile

"Smile, it's free therapy" – Douglas Horton. When you smile, your brain releases tiny molecules called neuropeptides. These happy hormones whizz around your body, improve your mood and help release negative emotions. Even a fake smile can legitimately reduce stress, lower your heart rate, block fear, and allow you to feel more confident instantly. So, slap on a smile and show up for your audience just like a showgirl does!

Glow Up

No successful showgirl is ever seen on stage without a costume. It's natural to feel vulnerable in the spotlight and trying to hide from the eyes of others when you don't feel confident often leads to dulling down our own light, wearing dark colours and generally hiding in the sidelines of our own life. Why not hide instead behind a costume of colour and curated confidence? The colour psychology is that different colours can evoke different emotions and impact how confident others perceive you. It's a trick the entertainment industry has used in shows and situations for decades and it's one you can very easily adopt in your day-to-day clothes and glow up.

Focus

I promise you all performers feel nervous before stepping on stage. The difference is, in those fleeting few seconds just before the curtain rises or the camera rolls, I can assure you they are, "Speaking to the desire NOT the fear." In order for any performer to push through doubt they must and will be focusing those last important thoughts on what will go right, what they will be rewarded with, what it will feel like to succeed. And you must too. Train your brain to focus on what you want and will achieve with the confidence you desire to have and see what results and new confident heights your new growth mindset will reach.

Practise the above tips and tricks daily. Use the hacks I have shared with you to fake it till you feel truly safe to show up and most importantly find the right community, supportive people and space that make you feel safe.

Safe to Show Off

As I stand in the spotlight on an international stage speaking to an auditorium of people waiting to hear what I have to say, I am confident thanks to my stage school dance and drama training, but more importantly, I am confident thanks to my community. Real people in the real world with whom at every stage of my life I have formed real connections and can see and feel their unwavering belief in me.

Never underestimate the validation and influence on self-esteem that comes from socialisation and support. The internet has its benefits and social media is an aspect of business we cannot ignore, but in-person and face to face is where I urge you to be. Building genuine connections and relationships inside real life communities should never be overlooked. The right people, your people, WILL celebrate you and want you to shine and succeed and with every positive reinforcement, connection, and conversation your confidence WILL grow.

In a world where so many people seem to favour independence and autonomy, I am grateful for my collaboration over competition nature and the deep-rooted commitment to being part of, and creating, communities.

When it feels safe to 'show off' you know that you are in the right circle, the right space, the right spotlight, and the right community. Then and only then will you stop hiding, show up like a showgirl, and confidently shine in the spotlights of your life.

Whether you are an aspiring or established entrepreneur, have lost your confidence or not, I invite you to join my community; PerformerPreneur. If this chapter has unlocked your inner showgirl and you find yourself feeling aligned with my mission to help others feel safe to show off, then let's make plans for me to deliver my keynote to your community. I'd love to share my entertainment industry energy and confidence gold in-person or online for you.

POWERHOUSE

Karen Nicholson

About the Author

Karen is a Story Work and Mindset Coach having been accredited with Andrea Callanan and her Aligned Coaching Academy and the Institute of Management and Leadership. A Certified NLP Coach and Practitioner with INLPTA and a Certified mBit Coach and Laughter Yoga Leader.

Karen Empowers individuals and groups to find Joy in their life and to discover their Authentic, Heart-Led, Compassionate, Courageous and Creative Self in life, at work, as parents, and in business.

Before embarking on this new coaching path as the 'liberator of the human spirit to create a wiser world,' Karen was a health professional for over 36 years. During that time, she worked as a RGN an RMN a Public Health Nurse and latterly as a Health Visitor with a special interest in Perinatal and Maternal Mental Health. In this role Karen held space for and empowered thousands of parents to make choices in respect of their own and their children's health outcomes.

Karen is a wife to Paul, a mum to Daniel, a mother-in-law to Sophie, and a proud Nanna to two beautiful granddaughters, Zi Xuan, aged ten, and Zi Luo, age eight. She has a fur baby, Jasper, a border collie who is seven, who loves meeting people and eating cheese.

Karen is a daughter to Stanley (1931 - 1999) and Sparkly Margaret the co-founder of Jars of Joy CIC without whom she would not be here today. Thanks Mum and Dad x.

Karen is available for one-to-one and Group Coaching, Speaking Events, Corporate events and workshops in a variety of settings.

Jars of Joy CIC was recently Highly Commended in the Wyre Council Community Awards and a finalist in the Wyre Business Awards for contribution to the Community as a Non-For-Profit Organisation.

Please consider this as your invitation to join our conscious community of Joy.

Email: Karennicholson@me.com

Website: www.jarsofjoy.co

Social media:

www.facebook.com/groups/278367259900353/

0-60 in a Chapter

Sixty trips around the sun. It's a milestone, a testament to the resilience of my spirit, the strength of my body, and the courage of my heart. I stand here now, not just as a woman who has lived six decades, but as someone who has thrived, endured, and risen stronger with every challenge. I am powerful, resilient, and brave. I am a woman who knows her worth.

This moment in my life feels like a celebration – a celebration of the battles fought, the lessons learned, and the wisdom gained. Turning sixty is not an end; it is an awakening. It is the realisation that my journey is far from over, and I hold the pen that writes the next chapters. I've reached an age where I no longer ask for permission to live authentically. I live on my terms, guided by the innate wisdom that has carried me through life's trials.

In this season, I embrace my courage to create, my power to heal, and my strength to inspire. Every scar tells a story, every wrinkle holds a laugh, and every memory whispers that I am still here – strong, unshakable, and ready to soar into whatever comes next.

My story begins on the 8th of October 1964. I entered this world prematurely, arriving earlier than expected and smaller than most, but with a will to survive that would define my life. I remained in hospital for several months after my birth, under the watchful eyes of nurses and doctors, fighting to grow stronger every day. I was born a delicate child in many ways, but one who was deeply loved and wanted.

Even now, I feel immense gratitude to my parents. My mum and dad longed for a little girl, and their joy when I arrived was palpable, despite my early struggles. I wasn't meant to be here – at least, that's what the odds would have said – but I was. My mother's pregnancy hadn't been straightforward. For almost twenty weeks, her symptoms were dismissed, but she knew otherwise. She believed in what she felt, and I believe that stubborn streak she showed in refusing to give up on me became a part of my DNA. The resilience I demonstrate with seeming ease today started right there in the womb.

The 1960s were a time when little girls were often expected to be 'sugar and spice and all things nice,' and I was no exception. I was the long-awaited girl, a child born into a family that had hopes and dreams for my future. My story, it seemed, had already been written by my ancestors, my parents, and my grandparents before I could even walk. There were expectations – spoken and unspoken – of how I should be, how I should behave, and who I should become.

But life, as I would come to understand, has a way of rewriting even the most carefully crafted narratives. My early years were filled with love, but they were also a time when I began to sense the weight of these expectations. Being a 'good girl' meant conforming to ideals that didn't always align with who I was inside. It wasn't always easy to live up to the image of the perfect daughter, the perfect child.

I spent much of my childhood learning to balance who I was with who I was expected to be. Even then, I had a fire in me, a quiet rebellion against the constraints that tried to shape me into someone I wasn't sure I wanted to be. That fire was my lifeline, though I didn't fully understand it at the time.

Looking back, I can see how those early years set the foundation for the person I would become. The fragile, premature baby who wasn't supposed to survive became the girl who refused to accept limits, who fought to find her voice in a world that often told her to be quiet. The resilience I now embody so effortlessly was born in those hospital months, nurtured by the love of my parents and the determination of a mother who wouldn't give up.

My arrival into the world may have been unexpected, but I've always believed that I was meant to be here. I've always believed that my story was mine to write, even when it felt like others were holding the pen.

Lockdown was a defining moment in my life – a time when my resilience was tested in ways I had never imagined.

While the world stood still, I embarked on a journey of transformation. It wasn't intentional at first; I didn't set out to completely reshape my life. But as the days turned into weeks and then months, I began to realise that this time of isolation was also an invitation to turn inward.

During lockdown, I made the decision to study coaching. At first, it was simply something to fill the days, a way to be productive while the world slowed down. But as I dove deeper into the work, I realised that this wasn't just about acquiring a skill – it was about me. My coaching journey began with my own story, peeling back the layers of my life to examine the pivots, the patterns, the traumas, and the limiting beliefs that had shaped who I was.

One of the biggest barriers I had to confront was a belief I had carried since I was eleven years old: that technology was for boys, not girls. This idea had been planted in my mind by society and reinforced by countless subtle and overt messages throughout my life. It wasn't until lockdown, decades later, that I realised how deeply this belief had influenced me. I had avoided technology whenever possible, convinced that I couldn't master it, that it simply wasn't for 'someone like me.'

Confronting this belief required me to do something I had never done before: question the stories I told myself about who I was. I had to ask myself where these ideas had come from, why I had held onto them for so long, and – most importantly – whether they were true. It was uncomfortable, even painful at times, to confront the ways in which I had limited myself. But as I worked through these questions, something began to shift.

I started to let go of the identity I had clung to for so long – the one that said I wasn't good enough, that I couldn't learn new things, that I wasn't capable. Instead, I began to build a new sense of self, one rooted in confidence and self-worth. I learned how to regulate my autonomic nervous system, calming the fight-or-flight responses that had so often dictated my reactions. I became more accepting of myself, imperfections and all.

As I delved deeper into coaching, I realised that this journey wasn't just about me. The tools I was learning, the insights I was gaining – they were things I could use to help others, too. But before I could guide anyone else, I had to live the process myself. And so, I did. I lived my coaching wheel, moving through each area of my life with intention, examining what was working, what wasn't, and what needed to change.

Through this process, I discovered something unexpected: joy. For so much of my life, I had been focused on surviving, on getting through the challenges and making it to the other side. But during lockdown, I learned what it meant to truly live. I discovered the pulse of joy, the quiet yet powerful current that runs beneath everything, waiting to be tapped into.

One story that stands out from this time is the moment I finally overcame my fear of technology. It was during a coaching session with a mentor, who gently challenged me to try something new. I hesitated, the old voices in my head telling me I couldn't do it. But something inside me – something stronger – said, "Why not?" I took a deep breath and gave it a try. It wasn't perfect, but it didn't need to be. The point was that I had done it. I had faced my fear and come out the other side.

Another pivotal moment came when I began to embrace my identity as a coach. At first, I felt like an imposter, like someone who didn't belong in this space. But as I worked with clients and saw the impact of my guidance, I realised that I did belong. I had something valuable to offer, not despite my struggles, but because of them. My story, with all its twists and turns, was my greatest asset.

Lockdown was a time of great uncertainty and loss for many, and I don't want to diminish the challenges it brought. But for me, it was also a time of growth. It was a period when I stepped into my power, shedding old beliefs, and embracing a new way of being. I became more confident, more grounded, and more joyful than ever before.

Now, as I reflect on that time, I see it as the foundation for the life I'm living today. It was during lockdown that I began to understand what it means to live authentically, to align my actions with my values, and to prioritise joy. It was during lockdown that I became the person I was always meant to be.

The journey wasn't easy, but it was worth it. And as I continue to grow, I carry the lessons of that time with me. I know that resilience isn't just about bouncing back; it's about growing stronger, about finding meaning in the challenges, and about discovering who you truly are.

The heart of my work, my 'business gold' lies in the life I have lived and the lessons I have learned. My story is my foundation – a story filled with pivotal moments, patterns, and traumas, but also resilience, growth, and transformation. It is a story that was written for me before I was born, shaped by generations before me. Yet, it is also a story I get to rewrite every single day.

One of the most profound lessons I've learned is that the stories we tell ourselves can either hold us back or set us free. For years, I believed a limiting narrative: that technology was for boys, not for girls. This belief, planted in my mind as a child, shaped the way I approached challenges, often convincing me to stay small, to avoid risks, to doubt myself. But through self-examination and intentional work, I learned that these limiting beliefs do not define me. I discovered the power of choosing new stories – ones that empower rather than constrain me.

This is where the magic of coaching comes in. Through coaching, I explored my past with curiosity rather than judgment. I examined my traumas, my pivots, and my patterns. I began to understand how these experiences shaped me and how I could use them to grow instead of letting them define me. Coaching taught me that confidence isn't something you're born with – it's something you build, brick by brick, by showing up as your authentic self every day.

Central to my coaching philosophy is the concept of self-worth. Believing that you deserve good things is not selfish; it is essential. When you start from a place of self-worth, everything else begins to fall into place. I also learned to regulate my autonomic nervous system, a skill that has been life changing. Simple techniques like balanced breathing can shift you from a place of stress and overwhelm to a state of calm and control. When you're in the driver's seat of your own nervous system, you're in the driver's seat of your life.

I've lived the process of moving from stuck to liberated, and I know it's possible for anyone. It starts with exploring your story, accepting yourself for who you are, and healing from the past. Coaching can be a powerful tool in this process, as can frameworks like the 'Five Ways to Wellbeing,' which emphasise connection, mindfulness, learning, activity, and giving. These practices helped me find my way out of dark places with my mental health – places I've visited more than once in my life.

Ultimately, my life revolves around two core principles: gratitude and joy. Gratitude grounds me, reminding me of all the good in my life, even on hard days. Joy sustains me, and I've learned to anchor in it, to schedule it, to make space for it. Writing a 'joy list' and intentionally weaving moments of joy into my day has been transformative.

Karen's Business Gold

The wheel below I have lived and now share with others is not just about surviving – it's about thriving. It's about finding who you truly are, stepping into your power, and writing the story you want to live. And the best part? You get to rewrite it every single day.

Coaching Wheel

- Self-Acceptance & Love
- Mental Health
- Regulation of the Autonomic Nervous System
- Joy
- Self-Worth
- Story
- Confidence
- Limiting Beliefs

Your story may have been written long before you were born, shaped by generations past, and influenced by the circumstances of your upbringing. But here's the truth: every single day, you have the power to rewrite it. Your life is your story, and you are both the author and the protagonist. You get to be the change breaker, the cycle breaker, the one who says, "This is where it stops, and a new chapter begins."

The process begins with understanding the story that has been handed to you. Maybe it is filled with limiting beliefs, inherited patterns, or societal expectations that no longer serve you. You have the power to challenge these narratives and decide which ones to keep, which ones to rewrite, and which ones to leave behind. Your past does not have to define your future. Instead, it can serve as the foundation for the person you are becoming.

Stephen Covey beautifully encapsulates this idea in *The 7 Habits of Highly Effective People* when he says, "I am not a product of my circumstances. I am a product of my decisions." This powerful truth reminds us that we are not bound by the conditions around us; instead, we hold the responsibility and the freedom to make choices that align with our values and vision for the future.

Covey also emphasises the importance of proactivity, stating, "Proactive people recognise that they are responsible. They don't blame circumstances, conditions, or conditioning for their behaviour. Their behaviour is a product of their own conscious choice, based on values, rather than a product of their conditions, based on feelings." This perspective shifts the focus from external factors to the internal strength and agency we all possess.

Being the author of your story requires courage and self-awareness. It means taking responsibility for your life

– not in a way that blames or shames but in a way that empowers. It means identifying the patterns that no longer serve you and intentionally choosing to replace them with habits and beliefs that do. Covey's *Seven Habits* provide a roadmap for this process, from being proactive to setting goals, prioritising what truly matters, and living with integrity.

To rewrite your story is not just a one-time decision but a daily commitment. Each day presents an opportunity to live with intention, to choose gratitude over resentment, growth over stagnation, and joy over fear. It's about anchoring in the belief that you deserve good things and creating space for those things in your life.

Your story is not static. It is dynamic, evolving as you grow, learn, and transform. And as Covey reminds us, "You must decide what your highest priorities are and have the courage – pleasantly, smilingly, unapologetically – to say no to other things. And the way you do that is by having a bigger 'yes' burning inside."

So, dear reader, it's your story, and you get to write the next chapter. It starts with you – your choices, your beliefs, and your determination to live intentionally. Take the pen and begin.

POWERHOUSE

Donna Amos

About the Author

Donna Amos is an award-winning Family Law Solicitor and Director at Barker Booth & Eastwood – a well-established law firm in Blackpool. With a focus on helping families navigate the challenges arising from divorce or separation, Donna also assists clients in laying strong foundations for their relationships through prenuptial and cohabitation agreements.

Since qualifying as a Solicitor in 2007, Donna has specialised exclusively in Family Law. Her proactive and straight-talking approach is complimented by her ability to build genuine rapport with clients, many of whom are facing highly emotional and difficult circumstances.

Outside of work Donna enjoys staying active through running and fitness, as well as spending quality time with her family, her children, and her spirited boxer dog.

You can reach her at:

Email: donnaamos@bbelaw.co.uk

Website: www.bbelaw.co.uk

Social media:

www.linkedin.com/in/donna-amos-4036213a/

Seat at the Table

As I took my seat at the table at the National Law Conference, I calmly looked across the room at the other law firm owners with excitement for the day ahead. In the room there were partners of law firms with over 750 staff and Family Lawyers for the higher echelons, who hand-pick their high-net-worth clients. There I was, sitting amongst them at the same level. My younger self wondered how I would ever earn my seat at the table of such esteemed company. I left my self-doubt, which crept in intermittently, at the door and as the day unfolded my sense of achievement and belonging was clear and I allowed myself to let go of the self-doubt from my past of not being good enough or intelligent enough.

The breaks in between the Q&A panel sessions allowed me to share my ideas, be curious and be brave enough to ask questions of my peers and discuss topics with complete confidence. Following the sessions, I was seated for dinner with co-owners of a London based law firm and their finance director. I exuded such confidence, happily and knowledgeably discussing the day-to-day challenges of running a law firm and felt a sense of satisfaction and reassurance that I am indeed making a positive difference to my firm, our staff, and our clients. I can now see that I am a Powerhouse and deserve my seat at the table, but this was not always the case.

'Dad, have I failed?' I asked nervously as I climbed into his car after a long day at primary school. My friends whose post had arrived that morning before school shrieked and hugged throughout the day, vocalising their joy and excitement of securing places at Grammar School. By contrast, I spent the day with a sinking feeling in my stomach that I had failed my 11+ and wouldn't be joining my best friends at the senior school which we all hoped to attend. My dad carefully chose his words when confronted by my direct question, which possibly took him by surprise, and calmly and sensitively informed me that I had not passed. When I arrived home, I sat in the bathroom crying quietly whilst being comforted by my mum.

Many people would look back and carry this 'failure' with them in life, but what if believing that I had failed at the age of ten was just what I needed to succeed in life? My parents certainly didn't see me as a failure, but was I? This early 'failure' could have easily instilled limiting beliefs, but I had a different narrative, that no matter what doors were closed to me, I would create my own opportunities and create my own seat at the table. Even at such a young age I was an exception to the rule.

My parents' unwavering support continued throughout my education when I 'messed up' my A Levels. Not getting the grades I needed meant that I was unable to study a LLB Law Degree at my first-choice university. I was told by my teacher that I could still study Law but wouldn't be accepted into a traditional 'red brick university' and would have to go elsewhere. This further huge disappointment spurred me to take action and again create my own opportunities. I wasn't willing to accept this change to my life plan, so I proactively contacted the university to find a way to attend. With a change of my degree course to Law and Psychology, I joined my first-choice university and moved forward with my career aspirations and life plan on a different track.

I loved university, particularly the social aspect, but I didn't love my course. It wasn't the Law degree that I had wanted to embrace. At the end of my degree, results day ignited the same feeling of dread and poignant regret that I felt at age ten. I already knew deep down that I had not achieved the grades to put me on track for a 2.1 degree, which was the entry requirement for most law firms offering training contracts to aspiring solicitors. My gut feeling was right, and my 2.2 degree was jokingly called a 'Desmond' after Desmond Tutu, and I worried that I wouldn't be taken seriously.

Yet again, my pathway to success felt like a game of Snakes and Ladders, taking a few steps forward and then sliding down with obstacles to overcome. However, my tenacity, grit and determination ensured that I dusted myself off and kept looking forward. It wasn't the course I wanted, and the grade didn't reflect my true ability, but there were many positives to my time at university, including meeting my husband and friends who I remain very close to.

Following my degree, I continued with postgraduate courses at Law College, not giving up on my dream career or allowing my earlier academic grades to stand in my way. Here it became even more obvious that I would need to create a seat at the table for myself and I was more determined than ever.

On my postgraduate course, I met my best friend, and I was at last studying the subjects that I wanted to embrace when I started university. Had I not 'messed up' my A Levels, we would never have met, and if I had listened to the teacher who told me to go to a different university, I would not have met my husband and have my two wonderful children. I studied hard and began at last to achieve results and grades that I was proud of. I was no longer messing up. But I still had niggles of self-doubt – how on earth was I going to secure a training contract to become a qualified solicitor? I felt haunted by my prior results, but my resolve to create my own opportunities remained.

I was determined to get my foot in the door and be seen by law firm owners to show them what I could offer and that I would be an asset to their firm. Instead of seeking a position with a large corporate law firm, which I may have leaned towards had my grades been better, I had to hunt out and find my place. My summer of work experience at a range of firms gave me real exposure and insight into different areas of law and I instantly knew that Family Law was for me. I loved the client contact, personal connection and realness of Family Law and knew I could make a difference to people's lives by specialising in this area. I was subsequently delighted to be offered a training contract at one of the firms where I had undertaken work experience.

During my training, the local Law Society invited applications for 'Trainee Solicitor of the Year.' I contemplated whether to apply. Was I a worthy nominee? After a brief hesitation I asked myself, "What is the worst that can happen?" I went for it and submitted my application, supported by references. A few weeks later at the Law Society annual dinner, in front of a room full of lawyers from firms across the town, my name was called out as the winner of the award.

Fast forward a couple of years and, still living with pre-conceived ideas about 'success,' I believed the gold star was to secure a job at a large multi office firm offering corporate and commercial services alongside personal services such as Family Law. I secured a position and moved to a larger firm. Despite the story I had previously told myself that I would never get my foot in the door of a firm like this, I did so with resilience and passion for my work. My yearning for this idealised version of success did not match up in reality.

Having taken the step to move to a large law firm, I felt the drive and ambition within me to become a partner and business owner, but eight years on, and with a second child on the way, I felt that achieving this dream was not becoming my reality. The restraints of working in what felt at times like an inflexible environment wasn't aligned with what I needed, and mum guilt began to creep in. I didn't feel trusted to manage my own time and missed important school events. I knew something had to change. I began to seek new opportunities whilst on maternity leave.

I had achieved the first goal that my younger self wanted but again was back playing Snakes and Ladders. I began to wonder if moving back to a smaller law firm with opportunities for progression was in fact the ladder to my ultimate gold star. Yet again I was in charge of my own fate. I questioned whether I may regret such a move, and would it be a step back? What if I took a chance and climbed one rung closer to earning that seat at the table? I had to be brave, believe in myself, create my own opportunities, and take the risk.

I booked the last day of my notice period as annual leave so that I could watch my daughter play Mary in her first school nativity play. Sadly, I was robbed of this when she became unwell following her performance the day before, which my parents watched but I was unable to watch due to work. I can't get that time back again, but I now take responsibility for managing my own time and attend milestones in my children's lives without fear of judgement or rejection and support my colleagues to do the same.

Two years into my new employment, I knew I had made the right decision to move firms, but was I ready to become a business owner and back myself? The niggle of self-doubt asked, "Should I become a director first without the financial commitment of becoming a business owner and shareholder? What if I have nothing to say around the board table? What if I am caught out?" A pivotal moment arose when I rang my older brother for advice. Without hesitation, he told me to go for it, step up and become a co-owner of the firm at the earliest opportunity. This positive proactive view and encouragement was echoed by my parents, my biggest believers, and I walked into work the following day and boldly informed my head of department that I wanted to become a co-owner now, not in the future, and that's exactly what I did.

Two years into being a business owner, I stepped up another gear and became head of the Family Law department on the retirement of my former colleague and friend. The retiring director is a Powerhouse and spearheaded the department for many years before I joined. By coincidence she also has a 'Desmond' grade degree. Unlike me, she has always been proud of her degree certificate, as she viewed it as a necessary step to becoming a partner in a law firm and proudly had it on display on her office wall for clients to see. By contrast, I have never had my degree certificate framed or on show due to my personal belief that it is not something to be proud of.

When I pondered whether to put myself forward as a contributor for a book with the bold title 'Powerhouse,' I once again transitioned from feelings of self-doubt about not having an interesting enough back story, to asking myself, 'What would Marilyn do?' Marilyn is a formidable Family lawyer who grew a specialist Family Law firm. During my training, I looked up to Marilyn as an aspiring solicitor and admired her from afar. Whilst we never met in person, I followed her career and watched her give expert advice on topical issues on breakfast television. When I asked myself that question, I knew for sure that Marilyn would have been bold, brave and feel deserving of being called a Powerhouse and that sealed my decision to collaborate on this book. More recently I contemplated whether to apply for a Business Award after being nominated. There I was with the same feelings as when I was a trainee solicitor, hesitant about showing off and feeling the fear of not being worthy. Once more, I backed myself, supported by family, friends and colleagues and submitted the application. I was thrilled to be announced as the winner of the 'Professional Services Powerhouse Award' at the national Flamingo Business Awards.

Family Law involves working with clients who are navigating issues arising from the breakdown of their relationship. When advising my clients, I strive to reduce and manage conflict and avoid using inflammatory language when writing to their former partner or solicitor to avoid unnecessarily raising the temperature. Emotions are often already running high, and I don't believe it assists for solicitors to add to this by communicating with each other in an aggressive or confrontational manner.

I advise and support my clients through separation and divorce and ensure that they understand the options available to them and carefully consider the potential long-term financial and emotional consequences of their decisions. As a member of Resolution, a community of family justice professionals committed to working with families to resolve issues in a constructive way, I fully adopt their code of practice and use my experience and knowledge to guide my clients.

I listen to my clients with respect and without judgement, regardless of what issues or difficulties they have been through, and I find it rewarding to support and guide my clients though what often is one of the most challenging times of their life.

There are many misconceptions in Family Law and well-meaning family and friends often have something to say when a relationship breaks down, but in many cases their views or suggestions aren't in line with the legal position. Each case is different, and whether the breakup is amicable or not, it is incredibly important to have independent legal advice to ensure that you make the best decisions for you and your family.

Donna's Business Gold

In my experience there are some common myths in Family Law that can cause unrealistic expectations and lead to unfair outcomes which can have a detrimental long-term impact on people's lives. Some examples of these common myths are as follows:

Common Law Marriage

It is widely believed that if a couple lives together for a certain amount of time, they acquire the same legal rights as those who are married. This is a complete misconception. There are many legal differences between married couples and unmarried couples in relation to property, financial claims, and inheritance.

"I am divorced so my ex cannot make a financial claim against me".

Unless a final Financial Order has been made by the court, financial claims can remain open, meaning that your ex-husband or ex-wife could still make a financial claim against you in respect of income, capital, and pensions much later than when the divorce is finalised.

Prenuptial agreements are only for the rich and famous or a sign of distrust.

Many people choose to marry later in life and have acquired wealth prior to their marriage or may have children from a previous relationship or marriage that they wish to provide for. Rather than being perceived as a sign of distrust, a pre-nup can be a sensible step to have clarity and agreement as to how assets will be divided in the event of divorce. They currently are not legally binding. However, if prepared correctly, they can carry great weight in the event of divorce.

If your husband or wife had an affair, you will be entitled to a better financial settlement on divorce.

The Family Court's role is not to punish people for their behaviour during a marriage, but to ensure that the family's assets are shared fairly, and that the financial and housing needs of the parties and any children are met.

These common misconceptions often cloud expectations and so with my clients I give straight forward, easy to understand advice, free of legal jargon to ensure that they understand the options available to them and can make informed decisions. It gives me a profound sense of fulfilment to see the transition in the confidence of my clients and to be on the journey with them during such an important time in their lives.

Somehow by 'messing up' I am now a relatively young director and co-owner of a successful reputable law firm with a seat at the board table of fellow directors. My husband and I juggle the hectic balance of family life and our careers, and I cheer for my children at sports days and other school events and am present in both worlds. I didn't mess up. I made my success happen.

As an award-winning solicitor and regular attendee at the National Law Conference, I no longer feel like I am not worthy or deserving of a seat at the table. I have the confidence to be proud of my achievements and brush aside the niggles that have tried to disrupt my ambition in years gone by. I am sitting at the same table and leading the way with the big boys in the larger firms. Marilyn and my former head of department weren't intimidated by this, and neither am I.

What advice can I give to my younger self or others who haven't had a smooth journey to success? Be brave, take risks and believe in yourself. You are not defined by a grade because you have everything within you to create your own opportunities and seat at the table.

Maybe it is time to proudly hang my university degree certificate on my office wall after all!

POWERHOUSE

Chef Seema Dalvi

About the Author

Chef Seema Dalvi's culinary journey is a testament to the power of dreams, resilience, and the unyielding pursuit of passion. Born and raised in a Brahmin family, Seema faced numerous societal expectations that oven overshadowed her dreams. This stark disparity fuelled determination to prove that girls could achieve greatness in any field including culinary arts.

Despite these challenges, Seema excelled in her studies and extra-curricular activities, using every opportunity to hone her culinary skills. She learned from her nan, mum, friend's mums, neighbours, and street hawkers, finding joy and solace in every dish she crafted. Her passion for cooking remained steadfast, even as life took her down different paths.

After marrying her soulmate, Krishna, Seema became a secondary mathematics teacher. Moving to the United Kingdom brought additional challenges, including starting a new life and raising a family. Though she excelled in teaching, her dreams of becoming a chef never faded.

Determined to pursue her dream, Seema established Dalvee, her own restaurant in the UK. The journey was arduous, with moments of doubt and struggle. Yet her dedication and culinary skills shone through, turning Dalvee into an acclaimed restaurant known for its unique fusion cuisine.

Seema's story is one of unwavering determination and the courage to follow one's passion. Her journey from a girl with a dream to a celebrated chef inspires women everywhere to pursue their aspiration, no matter the obstacles. Chef Seema Dalvi is beacon of hope and an inspiration to all who dare to dream.

You can get in touch here:

Email: orders@dalvee.co.uk

Website: www.dalvee.co.uk

Social media: www.facebook.com/dalveepoulton

Live Like a Goddess and Do the Right Thing

|| श्री ||

Pronounced Shree – it signifies auspiciousness, wealth, grace, and prosperity. This word is mainly associated with divine feminine power, also known as Shakti meaning 'Powerhouse,' which is believed to be a source of all creation and the energy in the universe. This power is personified in various goddesses and, ultimately, all the women in this world who are revered for their strength, compassion, and nurturing qualities.

Introducing Chef Seema Dalvi, I am an award-winning chef and the owner of Dalvee Restaurant, and my cuisine embodies the essence of Shakti through my culinary journey and achievement. Just as a Shakti represents the creative force of the universe, as a chef, I channel my creativity into my own innovative and unique dishes. My ability to blend traditional Indian flavours with modern culinary techniques showcases my dynamic and transformative energy.

I grew up in Mumbai, India, a city that gives you strength from its multicultural, cosmopolitan aspect. I empowered myself by transitioning from a former secondary maths teacher to a celebrated chef in the United Kingdom. My journey reflects resilience and determination, qualities central to the Shakti concept. Shakti is often associated with nurturing and providing sustenance, much like how I nurture my patrons with creative dishes. My restaurant, Dalvee, is a place where I share my passion for cooking, creating a nurturing environment for my guests who are treated as

अतिथि देवो भव|

(Athithi Devo Bhavah), which means, 'The guest is God.'

As a chef and owner of Dalvee Restaurant, my role in the kitchen, and my recognition as the best chef of the year for the North of England at the 2023 Asian Curry Awards, highlight my leadership and influence in the culinary world. This was followed by the Top 100 Asian Restaurants in the UK.

Dalvee is a modern Indian fine-dining restaurant that prides itself on changing its menu every four weeks. The menu features fusion dishes from around the world alongside regional organic curry recipes from India. Our unique selling point is that everything is cooked fresh from scratch, with curries personalised to each guest's tastes. Given India's vast culinary diversity, one menu can't represent the entire country. Dalvee caters to a niche clientele – those who love rich flavours, fresh ingredients, and a truly delicious experience. It is a place where every guest is welcomed with a big smile and then return as family.

Now as celebrated Chef Seema Dalvi, my journey to becoming an award-winning chef and restaurateur was not without its challenges. Before I found my calling in the culinary world, I faced several obstacles that tested my resilience and belief in myself. I originally worked as a teacher in Mumbai. Despite my passion for cooking, I didn't initially pursue it as a career. The transition from teaching in Mumbai and England to becoming a chef was daunting and filled with uncertainty and self-doubt.

Being the middle child with an older sister and a younger brother, my arrival surprised my parents, who had hoped for a son. And this was the first challenge for me. People usually celebrate new arrivals, but not in my case!

Growing up as a girl in my society was tough. Back then, and even now in parts of India, boys are often preferred and seen as the ones to carry on the family lineage. That's one of the reasons in many parts of India, when the girls are born, they are killed. As a girl, I often felt the weight of these societal norms. My brother was encouraged to dream big and do whatever he would like to do but myself and my sister were subtly and sometimes overtly steered towards domestic roles. These narrow expectations deeply hurt my feelings and made me feel inferior, especially when

I compared myself with my brother, who had a freedom to chase his dreams.

Food and dance were the bedrock of my childhood dreams, guiding me toward a hopeful future in one of those passions. Life, however, had other plans. Despite completing my education, including university, I was told my path was predetermined: to marry, raise a family, and follow in the footsteps of the women before me. The weight of tradition was heavy on my shoulders. Feeling confined by societal norms, I channelled my frustration into determination. I am always thankful to my nan who encouraged me to be good in studies, good in dancing and cooking. Her encouragement helped me to give hundred percent in studies, extracurricular activities, cooking and striving to excel in every aspect of life.

I've always enjoyed assisting my mother, nan, and aunties since I was seven. The kitchen has always been my sanctuary, a place where my soul finds true happiness.

During my college and university years, I extended this passion by helping street hawkers and *Machi walis* (women selling fish). I loved learning new dishes, exploring diverse cuisines, and honing my culinary skills. I am profoundly grateful to all the women who helped shape me into the chef I am today. It's disheartening to see that when women cook, it's often seen as a duty, yet when men cook for family, friends, or guests, the process is celebrated as an art form. We certainly live in a peculiar world.

With considerable persuasion, my father finally permitted me to work after university. I began my career with private tutoring and a position at a bank. In between the phases of life, I met my soulmate, Krisha, for which life tested my resilience and my calling for true love yet again.

I compromised with my dream when my father didn't understand my aspirations and took up a job he chose. After marrying my soulmate, I became a secondary mathematics teacher. After moving to the UK, I faced additional challenges.

Upon moving to the UK, I got lost in the routine of teaching, housework and looking after my children. Earning money and fulfilling the usual dreams of buying a new house, car, holidays, etc, became my sole focus. In this new norm, I somehow forgot about my dream and started to compromise once again.

When we had children, they naturally become our priority. This was one more time I compromised with my dream, telling myself, "This is what life is." Yet my culinary skills never abandoned me, nor did the calling of my subconscious. Eventually, I was asked to conduct cookery lessons with the teaching staff and the students in most schools I worked at in my teaching career – a gentle reminder of the dreams I had once I set aside. In those moments, I reconnected with my passion, finding solace and joy in sharing my love for cooking. It was a reminder that dreams, even when deferred, have a way of resurfacing and bringing happiness when least expected.

During my teaching career, I served as a classroom teacher, then moved up to second in maths and acting head of maths, believing that everything would eventually fall into place and that I would love my career. One summer, my husband and I decided to raise money for the education of three girls in India and, to do so, I cooked for my neighbours, school colleagues, and friends over two weekends. The menu featured starters and main dishes from India, all freshly cooked and tailored to individual tastes. Those two weekends were a revelation for me – I was in my element and thoroughly enjoyed the entire experience. That lightbulb moment led me to leave teaching in December 2016, and by January 2017, I had embarked on a new journey as a personal chef.

Leaving a well-paid job to chase my dream of becoming a chef was daunting. As a little girl, I wasn't allowed to dream big as my parents had a different plan for me and my life, so my confidence was often shaky. Neither my family nor my husband's family members had ever had a business, which added to my doubts about pursuing this path at thirty-nine. But there was an inner voice urging me, "It's now or never."

I vividly remember my mother-in-law telling me, "You are lucky to follow your dream, so just go for it. Not everyone has the same skills as you do." Her words, along with my husband's unwavering support, became my pillars of strength. Their faith in me encouraged me to pursue my passion and believe in my culinary journey.

My husband and family were instrumental in my journey; their support and encouragement kept me resilient during tough times. I engaged actively with my community, sharing my struggles, and rallying support. My transparency, honesty and dedication resonated with many, helping Dalvee restaurant build a loyal customer base. Winning accolades like the, 'Best Chef of the Year for the North of England' at the 2023 Asian Curry Awards and becoming one of the top one hundred Asian Restaurants in 2024 validated my hard work and boosted my confidence. These recognitions weren't just personal achievements but a testament to my belief in my culinary vision.

When I was teaching in school, I often felt I was lying to students in my form by telling them to follow their dreams and passions. Yet I knew deep down that having faith in your dreams and surrendering to a higher power could make everything work out in the end. I wanted to set an example for all my students in my form, demonstrating that it's never too late to pursue your true calling. They saw first-hand how passionate I was about food and hospitality. By stepping out and chasing my culinary dreams, I aimed to inspire them to believe in themselves and their own potential. This is my testament to the power of dreams and the courage it takes to follow them, no matter the odds.

As a personal chef, I savoured every moment, gaining confidence and refining my culinary craft. I began hosting pop-up restaurants and vibrant Bollywood nights, creating memorable dining experiences for my guests. In 2019, I earned the prestigious title of, 'Best Chef in Lancashire' – a milestone in my journey. This accolade was not just a personal triumph; it significantly boosted my confidence, affirming my dedication and passion for the culinary arts.

After winning an award in 2019 and gaining confidence, my husband and I decided to pursue our dream project: opening a fine-dining contemporary restaurant. With a growing clientele, catering from home became increasingly challenging.

The idea of a restaurant took root, but COVID soon surrounded us. When I went to view the property on Breck Road, I remember telling the estate agent, "Yes, I would like to go ahead with this property," despite the initial expense being £5000 and having only £96 in my account. But with a strong mindset and faith, I believed everything would work out for me and Dalvee.

I faced many challenges, but my belief in myself and a supernatural power kept me going. Writing my first recipe book, 'Magikal Mumbai Flavours' was a crucial distraction from the difficulties during Dalvee's creation. We not only survived but thrived during COVID. Now, I proudly stand as a female chef and restaurateur in a male-dominated industry. To all the women out there: have faith in yourself and never stop chasing your dreams.

From my journey so far, I've learned that believing in yourself and your business aligns the universe to work in your favour, prompting you to take action. It sometimes feels like magic, but it's all about the energy and messages you project. Running a business taught me how to stay calm amid challenges. I purposely say 'challenges' instead of 'problems' because 'problems' feel negative, while 'challenges' motivate me to find solutions.

As I mentioned before, I had no prior experience in the hospitality sector before we embarked on our restaurant project. However, I reassured myself that with my sound knowledge of food, honesty, good communication skills, organisational abilities, and capacity to work under pressure – the rest I could learn along the way. And I did. I would also like to say that talking to the mirror every morning definitely helped me to boost my confidence, and I am sure it might help some of you.

Now, I am living what once seemed like an impossible dream. Like any family-run restaurant, we still face many issues post-COVID, but I've learned to take things one day at a time and handle each situation as it comes. My belief in myself, my product, and my service is why I still stand tall. When you stay true to your values, everything falls into place. Sometimes I feel stressed about a situation or see an undesired letter, but tapping always helps. I tap my heart and say out loud, "All is well" – a line from a Bollywood movie that has stuck with me for all the right reasons. After a few minutes, when I feel calmer, I face the situation head-on.

In the competitive landscape of Poulton's vibrant food scene, standing out is crucial. Dalvee has carved out its unique niche, and I'm incredibly proud of how the business continues to attract patrons both locally and from afar. The restaurant's adaptability to current trends has been vital. Over the past three years, I've become more creative in attracting guests through social media marketing, attending events, and engaging in business networks. These efforts have provided invaluable opportunities to connect with people and stay relevant and current in the market.

Seema's Business Gold

From my experience, I have learned that running my business is an art, blending creativity and strategy with perseverance and adaptability. Just like any masterpiece, it requires vision, passion, and the skill to navigate challenges with grace. Each decision and action is a brushstroke that contributes to the overall success and growth of the venture. The artistry lies in balancing innovation with practical execution, creating something unique and impactful.

When a woman steps into a male-dominated industry it often raises eyebrows. I felt the same when I became a chef. What I don't understand, though, is that when I'm in the kitchen, the pots, ingredients, and the cooking process don't recognise gender – they just result in delicious dishes. So why do we discriminate? My nan used to say that when men discovered the power of women, they got scared, leading to discrimination. Since then, we have followed the same trend of men being superior.

To summarise, I'd tell every woman, "Follow your heart, not the world's expectations. Pursue what you love and let the world see you shine. A woman's place is wherever she chooses to be. As a female chef, I wield my culinary skills with pride, breaking stereotypes and proving that passion and talent know no gender. Let the flavours speak, and let our stories be heard."

Live like a Goddess and do the right thing.

POWERHOUSE

Jennifer Parker

About the Author

Based in Manchester, UK, Jennifer Parker is a business owner and virtual assistant with over ten years of experience in administration and project management. Starting her career in the corporate sector, she has developed her skill set and earned her reputation as an Executive Assistant, managing complex projects and supporting self-employed professionals.

Prior to employment, Jennifer had a background in dance and performing arts and still continues to seek her interest in musical theatre. She also enjoys a variety of music genres, weight training as part of her commitment to a healthy lifestyle, and cares for her dog. She invests a lot of her time into self-development and reading books on personal growth and business.

Since 2021, Jennifer transitioned to virtual assistance to focus on delivering flexible, high-quality support tailored to the unique challenges of running a business.

You can contact Jennifer directly to find out about how her business can support you and to book a complimentary discovery call.

Email: jenniferparker@jp-va.com

Website: www.jp-va.com

Social media: www.instagram.com/jenniferparker_va

Never Settle

Aged thirty-one, I have everything I want in life, but this is not what society told me I needed to achieve.

I might not have what society deems expected by the age of thirty, but I do have my own business and am a shortlisted business awards finalist; and my message to you is... never settle. Living by that motto, I have gone against the grain of security, solely established a full-time self-employed income and am a fully independent homeowner. In control of my life, I am taking on new opportunities and pushing myself beyond anything I thought I would be capable of. It's easy to say this now, but it wasn't easy to get to this stage. There were a few obstacles in my path which I have had to overcome and, of course, learn from starting in my late teens and, to be completely honest, I wouldn't be the person that I am now if I hadn't been through the trying times that have made me who I am today.

If I could go back, I would tell my younger self this. Don't think, just do. You are more than capable of anything; self-doubt is the only thing standing in your way. Be cautious of who you let into your life as not everyone you meet has good intentions and leave any situation as soon as happiness starts to deplete. You're doing the right thing, even though it hurts; discomfort is temporary. The pain of staying where you are is worse. You'll feel like you've lost your way after stage school, and the confidence you had will be lost too. But it won't be forever.

My expectations of myself at this milestone in life are a little different to the 'norm.' Not long after I turned twenty-eight, I decided to use the skills I already had to delve into the uncertainty of self-employment and launch my own virtual assistant business and have been full-time since March 2021. I was lost when it came to careers advice, and I feel like I fell into my career path as the options presented to me at the time were an apprenticeship in administration or training to be a mechanic. After leaving stage school at eighteen, a decision I didn't take lightly, due to injury, I didn't know which way to turn and enrolled into the standard nine-to-five lifestyle.

Let me take you to the hardest lesson I ever learned. But I admit it has moulded me to be the best version of myself.

I was content with where I was at, given I had to step away from my dream career. I was in secure employment, who supported my training and development and my current education in a project management qualification. I felt like I had a route planned out for my career and a person alongside me that was also highly focused on their career. He was a few years older than me and was further on in his journey than I was, so I thought I had the right support and a sounding board to discuss business and what was best for me. Little by little, without realising, I was whittled down to become a quiet, obedient young girl, trying to progress with no confidence. He often dismissed my feelings and the humiliation I felt inside when I was laughed at when I cried and told I ruined his days when I asked for the bare minimum in a relationship. It made me question everything that I thought a relationship was, and myself. I'd never felt so afraid to express my feelings, as I wasn't sure what else I could be told to drag me further down than rock bottom. I completely lost my self-worth and that my feelings weren't valid. The person who I thought supported me, really couldn't bear to see me grow.

I can imagine many people have been in a very similar situation and can relate to the feelings that I should have seen the signs right from the beginning, and I kick myself for it. In the early stages of our relationship, I was hospitalised with sepsis, and he made no effort to check in on me (somehow, he managed to convince me to stick around!). Nothing like being told your organs were about to fail by the nursing staff to put things into perspective! I needed that wake-up call again, as the twenty-one-year-old girl who had her priorities straight from a life-changing experience was gone.

It was a family member, who wouldn't normally speak out, who noticed that I was spending a lot of time on my own in my bedroom, and when they eventually got the pain and hurt I was feeling out of me, they told me I needed to reconsider this relationship. My mental health had plummeted. This was the turning point, confirmation that it wasn't right, and I needed to do something for my own health. That relationship ended because I found the courage to speak up, and I self-referred myself to counselling.

I have no other words to describe the outcome of the counselling other than Jennifer 2.0 was born! It was the best thing I ever did. Never again would I be made to feel that way. I put myself first, prioritised my fitness, physically and mentally and travelled solo to see family abroad. 2017 Jennifer wouldn't have done that! Without going to the lowest point of my life, I wouldn't have become resilient nor have the confidence to stand up for myself when it is needed. I can still feel some vulnerability in me when I do, the fear of having someone tear me to shreds when I vocalise how I've been made to feel because of someone else's actions still gets to me at times, but I have worked on dealing with the intrusive thoughts to not let them win. Maturity is gained through experience, and this one was a major lesson in my life. Off the back of it I have learned about myself, what I do and do not want and is one of the biggest inputs into me believing in myself to set up my own business.

Fast forward four years and we were coming to the end of COVID; I think a lot of people re-evaluated their life during this time. Everything felt so uncertain, and I was confused with where to go next. I even looked at different career paths as I wasn't satisfied in my current one and I'd had a few bad experiences of treatment with previous employers, so was hesitant to go through another interview process. I'd always struggled to know what to put my time into, but was destined for more than what I was doing.

In 2021 I completed training at an academy where I learned how to use the skills I already had and launched a business, Jennifer Parker Virtual Assistant. Six months after launch, I secured my first client and could leave employment to push my new venture full-time. I was finally in a strong place; I had bought my first house with my then boyfriend and I felt I was on track. Unfortunately, that relationship also came to an end. I'd learned from the past not to stay somewhere I wasn't happy, and so upon agreement from both sides, it was best for us to go our separate ways. With that though came the stress of the sale of the house we had bought together. I moved back to live with my parents and it was a real shock to the system. The realisation I was nearing the age of thirty and, in terms of society, I had gone backwards. A huge milestone that should be celebrated was just a constant reminder that I didn't have everything together. I immediately started to compare where I was against others, and the people who gave me the disappointed look of judgement made me feel like I had let myself and everyone down. Along with that, moving from a house to a bedroom where I slept, relaxed, and ran my business was mentally straining, and there was nothing I could do to speed up the long process. It just added to the feelings of misery.

It was a constant state of small progress and then pulled right back for eighteen months. During that time, I could only control myself and so that was where I focused my attention. I kept my business going and prioritised my wellness. My health is still my number one priority; without it I cannot successfully achieve anything. I had to keep reminding myself that I wasn't the only person this would have happened to, it's just that we only really see the wins in people's lives and not what happens behind the scenes. I would get there at some point... near or far! I just needed to ride that wave of highs and lows and keep my sanity.

As difficult as it was, I'm proud I handled the situation much better than the way previous me would have. To think of that version of me all those years ago, who lost herself and all ambition in that relationship, is terrifying. The thought of the control someone had over me and the situation I would be in if I hadn't left is troubling. I've grown so much since then and in the best way I possibly could have, all because I found the strength to battle the mind games and take control.

The house sale finally came to an end! I got to the finish line, now own my home alone, got the closure on the relationship, and have a positive outlook because I'm in a better place to push my business and continue to grow in all aspects. I pride myself on my mindset and am passionate about maintaining this version of myself. My headspace is strong, and I am unapologetically disciplined with my priorities in my life. People noticed when I was low and again now that I'm winning! Energy is contagious and noticeable by others around you, which reflects whether or not you are on the right path and confirms the boundaries I hold now benefit me.

Societal expectations of marriage and parenthood by thirty have indirectly made people believe they have an entitlement to know what goes on in other people's lives. I've found that people subconsciously have no compassion or thought as to why people are where they are in their journey, because it's not what's seen as acceptable. We need to remember that not everyone's journey is the same as what they want. Being a parent may not be their be all and end all ambition in life. Some people may not be able to have a family. Marriage may not be an end goal. You don't have to explain why you aren't married, don't have children, or don't own a house. Not everything aligns with you and that is a valid answer, and we need to normalise not having to justify this.

The strength it takes to not go with the 'norm' in life should be celebrated and I will always accept the biggest compliment ever given to me being, "You are so certain about yourself." I will never again be in a place where I do not feel this is not adding value to my life. Do we think that staying in a relationship like one of my previous ones that dragged me down is acceptable? We live in a world where we would rather someone tick these boxes by the age of thirty because then at least we have the things we are expected to have by then. Well, I can tell you now at the age of thirty-one, not married, no kids, and no relationship, and I feel no pressure to have any of them. I am fortunate that I am someone who is very comfortable on my own (an introvert at heart) and have grown to be independent and make my own decisions. Even with my home, I have made the renovation decisions and done all the decorating myself, unless I've needed a fitting service (because, let's face it, I'm a business owner, not a joiner!). I'm now back in the space I wanted to be in years ago, just a little later in my desired timeline, and that's okay. No timeline is linear.

A final message that I would share with my younger self and that I want to share with you is that you can pull yourself through the toughest times and others do not have power over you.

Like me, you may choose to seek help and the lessons you learn will always be with you. You may leave future situations in life because you know to leave what no longer serves you, makes you feel valued or brings you joy. It's a lesson to learn, but the only person who will always be around you, is YOU, so you need to put that person first.

People will comment on where you are in your life and might ask you questions that will make you feel like you've made the wrong decision, but you've not. That's just their judgement of what happiness is. If my story can share one thing with you, it is that future you will thank you for choosing the discomfort of leaving situations rather than staying and not being true to you.

Choose yourself.

Never settle.

Jennifer's Business Gold

I have supported other entrepreneurs in their businesses to help them expand. When I first started working with one of my clients, they had a team of four staff and after two years they have expanded to a team of ten. When we first started working together, they didn't realise how much my role would support them and the benefits it would have.

Here's a quick checklist to see if you are ready to outsource your business in order to give you back hours that you can utilise to generate more revenue than the cost of a VA:

☐ Are you spending too much time on lower-value tasks? (For example, emails, scheduling, invoicing, data entry.)

☐ Do you have a growing to-do list that you can't keep up with? (You're missing deadlines/feeling overwhelmed.)

☐ Are administrative tasks taking time away from growing your business? (Your time is focused on marketing, sales, client work that doesn't directly generate revenue.)

☐ Do you know which tasks could be delegated to a VA? (You may know exactly, or you might need to note them down and have a conversation.)

☐ Are you ready to pay for support to save time? (No company overheads!)

☐ Do you have systems or processes in place for key tasks? (Generic or specialised.)

☐ Do you feel overwhelmed by customer support or client follow-ups? (Finding it difficult to respond promptly to client emails or customer queries.)

☐ Is marketing and social media falling behind? (Too busy to maintain a consistent online presence or execute marketing strategies.)

☐ Do you feel you could generate more revenue if you had more time? (You know if you could focus more on sales, networking, or product development, you could increase your income.)

☐ Are you ready to scale your business? (You're ready to take on more clients or projects but don't have the capacity to manage it all alone.)

If you checked any of the above questions, then you would benefit from introducing a VA into your business. Outsourcing frees up hours for revenue-generating activities, helps you manage your workload and helps you focus on business growth. By investing a short amount of time to discuss which tasks can be handled, onboarding and training/providing clear instructions, a VA can start smoothly. You will have more time to expand your business and for your personal life, therefore increase your revenue/give you a return of investment, and take part in personal activities that bring you joy.

POWERHOUSE

Ann Shirley

About the Author

Ann Shirley is a Chartered Financial Adviser and Director of Intergen Financial Planning Ltd, with over a decade of experience and whose effective and personal strategies and advice have helped clients from all walks of life. Recognising that each client has individual needs, Ann works to help each client to gain clarity, understanding and knowledge whilst helping to deliver achievable goals, understand choices and implement bespoke planning. She is particularly passionate about empowering female business owners and entrepreneurs and those who may have left the corporate world behind.

Ann also holds a Law degree from Brunel University of London and changed career from Legal to Financial shortly after having her two daughters. Supporting, advising, and providing guidance, research, analysing, and problem solving are all key to working within both professions and she utilises this skill set with each client.

In addition to providing one-on-one advice, Ann also provides financial wellbeing interactive seminars in schools, in workplaces and also universities as it's never too early or late to start on the financial wellbeing journey, and she strongly believes that everyone should have a level of financial literacy and also access to good financial advice.

As a woman from Liverpool, she and her daughters were born Evertonian and will as often as possible be at Goodison Park (soon to be at Bramley Moore) to watch and cheer on her beloved Everton; win, lose or draw. After all, Evertonians are born not manufactured. In the event that the football gets a little too much, Ann enjoys spending time with her family, her partner, her two amazing daughters and her three 'lively' dogs, creating memories and ensuring that work-life balance whilst taking care of her mental wellbeing.

Ann offers one-to-one appointments in addition to working with corporates and business owners alike to provide financial wellbeing workshops and bespoke advice.

You can reach Ann at:

Email: ann.shirley@sjpp.co.uk

Website: partnership.sjp.co.uk/partner/annshirley

Social media: www.linkedin.com/in/ann-shirley-8613998b

Breaking the Bias

As I write this, I am a forty-three-year-old Chartered Financial Adviser, and Director of my own Financial Advice Practice. And, whilst it seems still quite surreal to say, I now know I am achieving my own perceived success. The older I get (and the increase in inevitable grey hair and added fine lines) I have realised what my own idea of success is, and what's important to me.

Every single person has their own idea of what success looks like, and that's the magical part. My younger self would have strived for a multi-adviser gargantuan practice, or even a bit of world domination. When I looked at what I wanted, the important life qualities I wanted, things started to look very different.

For me, now, my success is my family, my own business and income in that order.

I have two amazing daughters and the most supportive partner and father to my girls. I have a business which embodies my values and beliefs and an income to support our way of life. Sounds a little too good to be true as I type these words, but this is a life I have created off the back of some interesting twists and turns, but a journey I am grateful for, as it brought me to exactly where I need to be.

A client called me recently and it's a call I think about often. We had our initial conversations, and I clicked with this client instantly, she was absolutely phenomenal in her outlook and zest for life. She met her absolute love of her life later on in her years, and her biggest fear was that they wouldn't see a thirtieth wedding anniversary. My client's parents had lived a full and incredible joyful life together since early twenties and she vividly remembers the immense love in the room when they celebrated their thirtieth wedding anniversary; this particular anniversary really stuck for my client.

Together we made this our plan; to bring forward her retirement. I am literally smiling ear to ear (think Cheshire Cat style) and bursting with pride, that through planning and some financial manoeuvring, my client and her husband could indeed begin to reduce her working hours and fully retire years before the anticipated age, and still be able to fully enjoy their retirement together as planned. My client called me, very emotional, around two weeks after we had reduced her working hours into a phased retirement as she had worked out that by starting a phased retirement and ultimately retiring early, that this has given them more hours, days, and years together. Upon adding these days up and comparing this to how much time they would have had together without the financial planning, meant that, all being well, she will absolutely get her thirtieth wedding anniversary.

Needless to say, we were both a little emotional, knowing what we could achieve: we could achieve her dream, a goal so personal and precious to her. My heart was full, I was absolutely thrilled for this wonderful couple, and I could burst with pride that I was able to bring this previously unattainable dream to life. This is why I do what I do, I am so privileged to be able help and share in life journeys, creating memories and helping those dreams, goals and ambitions come to life.

Presently, I am in my dream work life balance, genuinely helping clients and spending such precious time with family. However, this has not always been the case, such is life!

For over a decade I have been a Financial Adviser, and for a large proportion of that time I have been employed. Without question I adore my profession, and achieving clients' individual and broader family goals, helping them become a reality, for me has always been the buzz.

However, there came a time in my life which for me was that defining moment, the catalyst, which sparked a wave of fury, which I could not quell, and I knew the decision which I was to make would without question shape my life as it is today and my future forever.

I don't think its uncommon to at times feel riddled with self-doubt, the ever so present imposter syndrome, and listening to these nay-sayers too has all had its impact. How is it, that anything negative said or implied, even when we know it's wrong, we believe, and allow it to take up head space, yet all of my achievements and being able to positively impact and change people's lives doesn't seem to hold the same space, the doubt creeps in over and above this?

Being in a male dominated profession, I have always known I had push myself harder, to be assertive, always go the extra mile, it felt harder to be heard amongst the usually older dominating male figures in business. Dealing with this had been fine, it was okay, I knew the industry, I had developed a tough exterior to it, and being there for my clients made the journey worth it. I was used to the environment and navigated it well… well, that was until I no longer could!

Male dominance, due to the sheer volume of male advisers is one thing, however when this then crosses the border over into misogyny, well that's another thing altogether. When you are in the open office, all settled in for a quarterly update meeting, and the director strides in, in his pinstripe tailored suit turns and cheerily asks the only female adviser in the room to "pop the kettle on sweetheart." I literally froze, surely this chap wasn't the same who gave the speech when I joined that, "our firm is like a family, we all look after our own," or maybe that was the truth of the matter. For me this was the beginning of the start of the journey that would rapidly alter my career. This interaction was probably the lighting of the wick, the start of the slower burn before the catalyst which changed my career forever.

Over the coming months and ultimately years, the continuing of belittling behaviour, subtle at first, the 'banter,' the team meetings praising, 'us guys,' for achieving target, and being praised for fast asset grabs whilst being discouraged from 'fluffy conversations.' Being told that new business takes priority over reviewing client's objectives, being told I needed to be 'more shark' and less professional. Listening to advisers talk about the 'big clients' they landed, never considering a joint review to include their wife or partner, and when I asked why not, often the reply would be, Mr is the main Company Director and business owner, Mrs isn't worth the paperwork. Looking back, I do feel ashamed for allowing this type of 'culture' to continue, but I was told by fellow advisers, don't cause waves, it is what it is, they won't change, just you keep doing the right thing.

Unfortunately, this didn't end with the toxic work environment but had also seemed to be a little more widespread. I was invited to a select peer group 'Adviser Symposium.' This was a peer group for Chartered Financial Advisers to get together and discuss the changing financial landscape, possible legislative changes, and main industry news. Immediately what struck me as I entered the conference room, was that it was an entirely male populated room, not one other female adviser in sight. I was questioned by not one, but by three different male advisers all within a matter of minutes, asking me whether I am sure I'm in the right room, and did I know this was a room for selected financial advisers? I began to feel a wave not only of being utterly self-conscious but also followed by a tsunami of self-doubt, and, as the youngest person in the room, should I even be there? Were they right? What could I add? Should I just leave?

During this time, I kept reminding myself why I do what I do, not only to be doing this really important role, but to be visible in that role, sometimes we can't aspire to what we can't see, and I know I wanted this career, I have worked too hard to just walk away.

This next incident was the pivotal moment for me. It was during COVID, when a lot of people were furloughed, and my employer would love to run a 'quiz/training' on a Friday. Just prior to this meeting I had a call from my daughter's school, which always prompts me to panic, as I know they only call if there is an issue. They called to say that she had fallen badly whilst playing football, and that they couldn't say for certain whether there was a break, but best to get her up to hospital for a check. I felt sick, not only as my daughter was in pain, but as we were still in the midst of the pandemic and taking her into a hospital environment, the fear was horrendous, we knew so many people were suffering from COVID, and so much was still unknown.

I made the call to HR, who rightly told me not to panic, but if I could just call the director and let them know I wouldn't be on the meeting. As a courtesy, I did. This is where my initial fear turned to absolute rage, the words stuck in my head on a loop for hours and hours, "Oh Ann really, you need to really look at your priorities, clearly you are the breadwinner in your home and this meeting is so important, surely your husband could pick her up, think of your career, is it worth it?" It felt like my breath had literally been sucked from my lungs, I couldn't breathe, I was in absolute shock, my silence felt deafening inside my head, I simply could not believe what I had just heard.

All I could muster was one word, "Pardon?"

Again, the words were repeated in a similar phrase but at this point my head had turned from deafening silence to abhorrent rage, I felt my mouth move and say, "I'm going to collect my daughter." It didn't even sound like my own voice, but thankfully my voice had kicked in, somehow. I was left still in shock and reeling from this exchange, I was the most furious I have ever been in my life, my skin felt hot and prickly. I cannot remember ever feeling so incited with rage.

Wow, I mean, never in my life did I think I would be asked by anyone to pick a weekly meeting over my child, yet there it was. It was in that moment that I knew this was the very last straw, I was done. I had lost all respect for this company and those who made the decisions. I deserved more, my family deserved more, and my clients deserved more than this.

After returning from the hospital, it was clear that in addition to all the slow burning issues, this last one was the catalyst for me. I knew what I needed to do, it was 'now or never.' I handed my notice in, and I can tell you it felt absolutely incredible, it felt liberating and empowering and like a tonne weight had been lifted, I felt lighter than air. I knew this was the right decision for me.

What have you done? What are you going to do? How are we going to survive financially? We are still in a pandemic. How can you make this business work now? What if I fail? What next? These thoughts consumed me and whirled around my head, feeling like a hurricane of overwhelm.

What had I done? Seriously, what had I done?

I spoke to my partner and my amazing parents, who gave me their unwavering support. I spoke to my girls, who are always my biggest cheerleaders, and they reminded me of who I am and what I have already achieved. AND YES, I CAN DO THIS.

I knew I could, I knew I had the resilience that had built up over my working career. I knew I looked after clients in the right way, I knew with determination I could do this, I wanted to do this for my girls, to show them woman can succeed in a male dominated industry, you can do anything you put your mind to, no matter the obstacle. It felt right and I wanted to, actually no, I needed to succeed.

I established my business, and I can say that I have, without question, made the absolute right decision for me and my family. Was it easy? No, running a business is hard, but remember to look at your reason why, this will drive you forward when things are less than smooth sailing. Trust yourself, and don't let the self-sabotage and fear creep in. Allow yourself the space to believe in yourself and have the courage to do it your way, to achieve your version of success. Focus on your own goals, re-evaluate, and re-define, continue to grow your business in a way that is true to your values.

This is your business; your way and you are enough! If you are under-represented in your business sector, stand up, show up, be seen, let's break the bias. Surround yourself with other likeminded people who want you to succeed, and who will lift you up when you need a little extra nudge. You have got this; I believe in you!

In 2025, statistics are showing that over 60% of wealth will be in the hands of woman; the industry without question needs more female Financial Advisers. I adore that we are naturally inquisitive (or, if you ask my nearest and dearest, a little nosy). Combine this with understanding the dynamics and pressures faced by families, then overlay this with technical knowledge and what a Powerhouse Financial Adviser you are, or even to have in your corner. I would implore any woman who has an affinity in helping people, who loves to not only look at where people are now, but also where they have been (as this is often a window into a person's financial soul, as our thoughts and feelings towards money and wealth and financial stability are often formed from past experiences) and to come and join me in the financial world. I wholeheartedly believe that each one of us can make a difference, let's stand up and get visible, you never know who might be watching.

The world of finance for some can seem initially daunting and often fear of the unknown or what to expect can often be a reason that people may not seek advice from a professional Financial Adviser, and therefore I would love to share some of my top tips. This is a starting block to beginning the journey to financial freedom, which is entirely personal and undoubtedly looks different to each person.

Ann's Business Gold – Financial Top Tips

1 Know Your Income

Know exactly what comes into your household every month. For the employed, check your wage slip and make sure these are all correct:

- Tax code.

- Overtime hours logged correctly.

- Any deductions from the wage slip.
- Pension contributions.

For those who are self-employed: keep detailed records, invoices, contracts of work. If this isn't your forte, get a professional and work closely together.

2 Know Your Expenses

Be crystal clear on what are your essential bills (personal and business, but ensure they are separate), what you absolutely need to pay each month. Then look at where the rest of your income is going, break it down, there is no judgement in where you spend your hard-earned money, but give yourself the clarity to know where it is going. As a tip, try multiplying the figure you spend in a month by twelve to give you the annual spend, sometimes this gives a very different perspective!

3 The Eighth Wonder of the World

Albert Einstein is believed to have referred to compound interest as, 'The Eighth Wonder of the World,' and if you take just one bit of advice from me, tell your children about compound interest. Compound interest in a nutshell is earning interest (money) on not only the amount you put in but also on the interest (money) it makes, the longer it is invested, the more and more money it makes. Think of how you make a snowball. You start off with a little bit of snow and as it rolls along the snow it picks up more and more snow, the longer you roll the snowball the bigger and bigger it becomes.

This next task may surprise you. Look online for any UK compound calculator, and add a monthly amount of £200, for a duration of 45 years, with a 10% annual interest rate and then see what those savings are worth. The amount you would have invested would be £108,000 in total over those 45 years. For those who can't wait I will pop the answer below my Top Tip number 5!

4 Protect what means the most to you

This is especially important for those who are self-employed, for those who have children or someone who is dependent upon you. Financial protection such as insurances help ensure that you and your family or your business will be able to pay bills, maintain your lifestyle and safeguard your savings, should the worst happen. Life unfortunately often isn't fair, and rarely runs to our plan, curveballs can, and often do, come when least expected and can throw us entirely off kilter. The earlier this is in place, often the cheaper it is, but always review this area of financial advice as your needs will change over time and so do the policies. If in doubt get a Financial Adviser to make sure you have this correct.

5 Tax Relief

Tax rules can and do change, so it's important to know what you need to pay tax on and when. Equally, it's also paramount to know when you can get tax relief. The government will add an additional 20% onto a payment made into your pension, this is available to those who are in employment, are self-employed and even non-taxpayers. (There is a different rate for those who pay Scottish income tax.) For example, if you add £800 to your pension, the government will add a further £200! If you are a higher rate taxpayer, you can get up to 40% tax relief, meaning a £10,000 pension payment would only cost you £6000, and if you fall into the additional rate of tax at 45%, you can claim 45% tax relief. Imagine a pot of money that not only can get you an instant 20%/40%/45% increase on, but also then can benefit from compound interest over time.

This is so important for woman, as unfortunately we have what I refer to as our 'woman's tax.' We have so many life events which can impact our pensions and savings. If we choose to have children, then our pension contributions will be affected, as you take time off to have your child or children, you may decide to reduce your hours at work to have a balance between work and raising children, or simply to juggle the childcare costs, ultimately reducing your earnings and therefore pension contributions. Then we have the wonderful world of menopause and perimenopause in which many woman, due to their symptoms, have either left their current role, sought a part-time role, or even not applied for a promotion. Also, there can be additional family generational pressures. You may want to reduce hours to look after parents, grandparents, or grandchildren. We have all these factors to contend with. Knowing that you can boost your own pensions with the additional tax relief and compound interest, ensuring that with advice and clarity, you can make informed decisions on your present and future. I would encourage everyone to seek advice and let's start to bridge this gender pay gap.

Answer to the question in Top Tip number 3 – The Eighth Wonder of the World

£2,096,500.34.

POWERHOUSE

Debbie-Lyn Connolly-Lloyd

About the Author

Debbie-Lyn is an expert model manager who helps aspiring models from marginalised backgrounds to feel empowered, build resilience and navigate their way to becoming a successful diverse fashion model.

Before founding DL Models Ltd, Debbie-Lyn worked in the fashion, beauty, and entertainment industry for many years, as a professional makeup artist, plus-size model, and supporting actor for many well-known TV shows.

Since creating DL Models at the beginning of 2024, Debbie-Lyn has been using her expertise and extensive contacts within the industry to help launch successful careers for aspiring models, who have faced similar challenges in life as she did.

Debbie-Lyn is available for a free discovery call – just book through the website.

You can reach Debbie-Lyn at:

Email: debbielyn@dlmodelsltd.com

Website: www.dlmodelsltd.com

Social media: www.instagram.com/dl_models_ltd

Dream It, Believe It, Achieve It

As I look around the stunning art deco inspired ballroom dripping in crystal chandeliers and pure opulence, listening to the hauntingly beautiful voice of an opera singer's rendition of 'Nessun Dorma,' surrounded by my friends, celebrities, and philanthropists, it's difficult to believe that this is my life now. The ICON Awards and celebrity gala is definitely one of those 'pinch me' moments, and I have been lucky enough to have attended four of these events already, completely awe-inspiring and, at the same time, still somewhat surreal.

The success I have enjoyed increasingly over the past five years has seen me become a sought after professional published curve model, a body confidence advocate, and inclusive fashion designer. I have attended some of the most prestigious events and walked some of the most influential runways in the UK, including Liverpool, Manchester, York, and London Fashion Weeks. With a mission to increase visibility for plus size women in the mainstream media and fashion and beauty industry, I am the successful business owner of nationally acclaimed DL Models Ltd. We empower people who lack confidence to believe in themselves again, to feel represented, beautiful, and confident, and begin their journey to becoming successful diverse models.

I have built an extensive following on social media and been featured in the local and international news, sharing my story, and changing standards in the fashion and beauty industry. My life today couldn't be more different from where I began, the confident, optimistic, determined woman people see today is unrecognisable to those who knew me in the past.

I spent my early teenage years as an insecure, self-destructive, pessimistic girl, living life in victim mode, and suffering every day from the devastating effects of childhood trauma and sexual abuse. I left the family home as soon as I finished school and worked hard from the age of fifteen in different jobs to keep a roof over my head. I felt worthless inside and sought the love I had lacked through childhood in one abusive and toxic relationship after another. I struggled with my self identity and my body image massively, leading to disordered eating for many years.

I became a single mum at the age of twenty-three, having my first little boy, then I went on to have my daughter, and another son. I had always wanted to be a mum, but had never imagined being alone in my late twenties with three children, one who had a serious medical condition and two who were neurodivergent. It was more challenging than I ever could have imagined. I felt a huge sense of failure that none of the relationships with my children's fathers had worked out, and the stigma surrounding this absolutely ate me up.

When I met my husband after I turned thirty, I pictured the children's and my lives suddenly changing into what I had always imagined a family unit to be like. He was going to be my knight in shining armour who rode in, swept me off my feet, and finally gave me the security I craved. Sadly, there was no white picket fence, or happily ever after, but instead I found emotional and physical abuse, constant criticism and put-downs, and me seeking escapism at the bottom of far too many bottles of wine. I gave birth to my youngest son in the first year of our marriage, and I hoped and prayed that somehow having our own child would make our relationship better, but of course this wasn't the reality.

I was already isolated from my family and every day seemed like an uphill struggle, to which there would never be an end. I felt lost, alone, and deeply unhappy. Guilt also played a major role in the deterioration of my mental health and self-worth; I had everything I thought I had always wanted, everything I thought would make me happy, but it wasn't what I had imagined it would be at all. I reached the point where I lost all hope of ever feeling happy, and I believed my children deserved someone better than me, I hit my absolute rock bottom.

Waking up in the emergency room, surrounded by bleeping machines, I had two thoughts. Firstly, that my attempt to end it all had failed. Followed by the realisation that no one was sitting by my bedside.

I learnt later from the hospital staff that I had been brought in via emergency ambulance, after a friend had suspected I was in a bad way. I learned that I had lost care of my children, my home... everything, but even though I had tried, I had not lost my life.

I started to wonder whether there was a reason, perhaps my life did still have some potential? Perhaps as hopeless as things had seemed, I survived for a reason? This was my transcendence, the beginning of my healing journey, a deeper belief that I had purpose here. It sparked a desire to discover what life was meant to be all about.

My journey to finding happiness meant letting go of everything I thought a woman had to want in life, and the realisation that being a mum wasn't enough for me to be happy! I needed to also be myself. The only issue was that I didn't have any sense of who I was, apart from being an unhappy, resentful, single mum.

I set out on a journey of self-discovery, learning that my lack of self-confidence had stemmed from constantly being criticised growing up. The eldest of my siblings, I was also used as the emotional support for my mother from a young age in my parents' never ending war, which each year accumulated in threats of divorce, that I started to hope for, but never materialised. My choices in poor relationships, I would later learn, was typical of someone who was brought up in these circumstances, having little to no boundaries, lack of self-worth, and an unhealthy relationship model. I learned how to meditate to quieten the constant racing thoughts in my head. Sitting in quiet contemplation I began to see that I needed to follow my creative passions in life, I had always been creative since I was a child, and had always dreamt of becoming a fashion model, which I felt was out of reach due to my curvy figure. I also loved painting, experimenting with makeup looks, and drawing my own fashion designs.

As I progressed along my healing journey, I learnt a lot about how my childhood had moulded me, and I began some vital inner child healing work, which helped me to re-parent my inner little girl, using all the knowledge I now had, as an adult, and show myself the love and compassion I missed as a child, and hadn't been able to give myself through adulthood. My inner little girl, the creative child who had those big dreams, had been pushed down and criticised for long enough. It was time for her to be happy now. I learnt various coping mechanisms on how to process and deal with my own emotions. As a child, I had never been allowed to show my emotions safely, and I had become to adept at hiding them, I had no idea how to simply sit with my feelings! This was vital if I was going to be able to stop using alcohol as a crutch to dampen down my difficult emotions. I practised grounding techniques for when I was sitting with the big emotions so that I could resist the urge to sink into disassociation, and breathing techniques to calm my nervous system when I felt overwhelmed. Holistic wellness and self-care became my new normal, and what seemed so contrived at the beginning, ended up being second nature to me in time.

Once I reached a place of stability, my beautiful children came back home, I was overjoyed that I had been given a second chance to be a better mum, I vowed to make them proud of me and to build us a life where they no longer had to watch me struggle. I set out creating my own business around the things that brought joy to me, first qualifying as a professional makeup artist, and then venturing out into the glamorous world of fashion modelling. My confidence grew more and more as my makeup clients would send me their feedback, singing my praises, and telling me how good I had made them feel. I just loved the creative aspects of face painting and body art, learning special effects, and eventually teaching my skills to others in workshops.

Following my counsellor's advice to step out of my comfort zone, I went along to a model casting, which advertised specifically for curvy women, and when I was chosen for the African fashion themed runway show, my confidence absolutely soared. I met so many supportive women just like me, and I finally felt the sense of belonging I realised I had never had.

Healing from so much past trauma was an ongoing fight, and I would say that there wasn't one of these things I did which helped me become the woman I am today, but a combination of all of the counselling, holistic therapy, CBT therapy, addiction therapy, inner child healing work, and pushing myself out of my comfort zone into travelling alone and modelling on runways around the country, as well as photoshoots where I could really get in touch with my creative core – the perfect recipe for me to thrive!

After four years of working as a makeup artist within the fashion industry and modelling, I had built up extensive knowledge of the industry as well as an impressive network of industry professionals. I was lucky enough to be invited to incredible red carpet dinners and awards events, where I met some of my all-time favourite celebrities. I was travelling first class around the country, staying at five-star hotels, and having experiences I never thought possible for someone like me.

Although I loved every moment of my modelling career, I did notice that a lot of prejudice still exists within the fashion and beauty industry, with diverse representation leaving a lot to be desired. I wanted to challenge this, and help other people just like me, who had suffered from adversity throughout their lives. I wanted to show people how amazing life could be when you start to really believe in yourself.

I set up the business I now run, DL Models Ltd, a model management company like no other! I built a team of likeminded professionals, who are experts in the fields of counselling, inner child healing, holistic therapy, and modelling skills. We offer the incredible unique opportunity for aspiring models to join us, through a choice of memberships, ranging from our free Facebook community, 'Embrace,' which is all about inclusivity, diversity and celebrating each other's differences. Our members will find support, encouragement, and inspiration from each other, to enable them to live more authentically, embrace their uniqueness, and feel empowered. For anyone who wants to take the next step beyond the online community, they can join our paid subscription group, 'Shine,' which includes real world opportunities to meet up socially, network, apply for model castings, take part in some workshops, and join our models on opulent styled shoots, keeping the images for their portfolios, or join our one-to-one expert coaching programme, 'Rise,' to develop our clients' mind, body and soul, so that they have the resilience it takes to become a professional fashion model! We provide opportunities for them to travel and take part in networking events, social events, professional styled photoshoots, and runway shows, building up their confidence as well as their portfolio.

When I see the incredible transformations of our clients happening right in front of my eyes, I am always blown away. One client came to us who is neurodivergent, and suffers with PCOS, which causes uncontrollable bloating amongst many other symptoms. She was at the point of mental health crisis, and I could see my past self in her struggle. With our expert coaching team, I watched this wonderful woman transform from having no confidence, hating her body, and suffering from social anxiety, to strutting down the runway at our event, 'The Inclusive Fashion Show,' in front of a sold-out audience, wearing a white bikini and open kimono, absolutely glowing, and beaming a smile from ear to ear. She has since gone on to model for diversity campaigns, been published in magazines, and even featured on the BBC news article we were invited to do. This really is the most rewarding line of work for me, and it's all inspired by my own healing journey.

When I started believing I deserved a better life, realising and admitting that being a mum wasn't actually enough for me to be happy, and stopped trying to please everyone else but live authentically, it lifted so much pain, guilt, and feeling I needed to escape from my own life. I built a business and a life which I just love, and my children are so proud of the woman I have become.

DL Models Ltd has gone from strength to strength in its first year, we have clients from every area of the UK, having secured publications globally in top magazines like Global Woman Magazine, Lancashire Life Magazine, The Mirror, and Pepper Magazine, as well as booking our clients for runway shows such as Kent Fashion Week, and The Sustainable Fashion Show at Blenheim Palace. We have taken our clients on styled shoots like our bridal collaboration shoot at Allerton Castle, and proudly been nominated for ten awards, which is an incredible honour.

When I look at my children and how they are influenced by what they see in the media, I know how important my mission to increase diverse representation is if we want our next generations to grow up feeling validated, confident, and beautiful. In an industry traditionally associated with fashion models being very tall and super thin, I am looking to reclaim the meaning of what a model is! The term model is defined as, "A thing used as an example to follow or imitate," and that is exactly what we look for in our clients.

I stepped further out of my comfort zone recently, and set up my own Community Interest Company, to enable me to reach and help more people across the country, some of whom have been the most severely affected by adversity and are unable to afford our business services. It's so important that these people can not only access our services, and transform their lives for the better, but also to enable more powerful and inspirational stories to be told to future generations, that they matter and, despite where you start from, you should always dream big. The funding will allow our CIC clients to access much needed support, counselling, healing, and wellbeing workshops, building their belief in themselves as well as improving their mental wellbeing, and giving them chance to belong, something which was pivotal in my own healing journey.

I set out to find my purpose, but I found so much more: pride, confidence, friendships, direction, happiness, and a legacy to leave behind me when it's my time to go. I thought I was selfish for not being happy with just being a mum, but what I have given to my children is a happy mum, and the drive to follow their dreams too, unapologetically.

Debbie-Lyn's Business Gold

My three top tips to anyone facing adversity, and wondering what their purpose is, would be:

1. Find what makes your heart sing and then think how you can build your life and career around that.

2. Learn to live for the day you are in, doing one small thing each day which makes you feel proud.

3. Let go of anyone and everyone who doesn't inspire you.

My mantra at DL Models Ltd is what I tell my children every day, 'Dream It, Believe It, Achieve It.'

POWERHOUSE

Amanda Shearer

About the Author

Amanda Shearer is a dedicated Mortgage Broker with a passion for helping individuals and families achieve their dream of home ownership. With twenty-four years of experience in the mortgage and financial industry, Amanda brings a personalised, friendly approach to every transaction.

Her expertise and passion span a wide range of mortgage products, especially helping self-employed business owners navigate what sometimes can be a complicated area, as well as including first-time buyers, refinancing options, and investment property financing. Amanda takes pride in her ability to navigate the complexities of the lending process, ensuring her clients receive tailored solutions that fit their unique financial goals.

Amanda is committed to making the mortgage process smooth and stress-free. She works closely with a network of lenders to secure competitive rates and terms, empowering her clients to make informed decisions with confidence. Her approachable style and unwavering dedication make her a trusted partner in one of life's most significant financial decisions.

Amanda enjoys walking her dachshund Lulu and her cavapoo Betty, travelling and baking.

Contact Amanda Shearer today to discover how she can help make your homeownership goals a reality.

Email: amanda@mismoneypennymortgages.co.uk

Website: www.missmoneypennymortgages.co.uk

Social media: www.facebook.com/amanda.shearer

Finding Miss Moneypenny

Driving along on my way to visit a friend on a cold crisp October morning, playing my favourite tunes, my head was buzzing with ideas. I was yet again at a crossroads in life and had come to a decision. Earlier that week, I had to leave the comfortable office environment that I had grown to love, and my choice was to stick with a safe job or twist to a new challenge and go it alone in business for the first time.

I loved my job, but where I was working had changed over the years, from a small, close-knit business run by a truly inspirational gentleman. It was now growing and losing its happy environment and had become toxic in certain areas of how it was being run. I knew that this business didn't have my client's best interests at heart, they wanted to control me by making me charge ridiculous fees. I felt uneasy; this didn't sit well with my values. It was having a detrimental effect as I couldn't justify the extortionate costs. Long term, I would lose my clients, so I knew I had to make that decision to leave. It was the push I needed to make a big jump out of my comfort zone.

As the music played and I hummed along, driving down that autumnal road I made the decision. Out of nowhere, came the name Miss Moneypenny, and I knew that I needed to make it happen. It was there and then at nearly fifty that I claimed my true passion to do it my way, on my terms and created Miss Moneypenny Mortgages. After a lifetime of being dependent on others in life and business, it was my time to step out of my comfort zone and become my own Powerhouse as a financial expert and mortgage advisor.

I had all my clients, my knowledge, the skills to do it for myself, there was nothing stopping me. I was just fighting my demons of staying in my comfort zone, sticking to what I knew. Life is too short, and I felt unable to do my job to the best of my ability in this environment.

I finally knew what I wanted for the first time.

Looking back, I was always drifting. I was bright at school, but never had any direction or ideas of what I wanted to do. My first job was a record librarian at Red Rose Radio in 1988 in Preston. This wasn't a 'real' job. I was so lucky going to work, listening to music every day, sorting out the records for the shows, and going to the album launches in London, mixing with celebrities of the time, which was amazing. That job was not going to last forever, as records began to be phased out and CDs took over the industry began to change. Looking back now, I got to make some amazing memories and made lifelong friends. I gained valuable skills throughout this time which have stood me in good stead for the rest of my life.

I was working in a predominantly male environment and had to stick up for myself and adapt to situations very quickly. Highlights of my first job were meeting my husband and being able to meet some amazing people. One of my favourite memories must be meeting Celine Dion, which I was lucky enough to do backstage after a show, and having a cup of tea with her.

Life was a roller coaster, and in March 1996 I found out I was pregnant. Despite my joy, I was so sick, and I felt ill for nine months; this being the main reason why I only had one, I could not have done that again. Daniel was born in October 1996, and we got married the following year. I found myself living in Sheffield, as my husband was then working for a radio station there.

I was thrown into a world of nappies and sleepless nights, a far cry from my nights on the town and meeting celebrities. But I loved being a mum, and it's been my proudest achievement.

I was lucky enough to be able to devote my time to him, and I spent the first three years being a full-time mum, but to be honest I felt trapped. I was jealous of my husband as his life didn't stop like mine. He had a successful career, he was out all the time in Manchester and London, flying around the world whilst I sat at home. I felt I wanted more and, for the first time in my life, I felt like I was missing out.

I had no career, I was sitting at home but significantly I hated being dependent on someone and having to ask for money as a non-working mum. I felt I had lost my freedom.

Not being financially free made me feel trapped and frustrated and, looking back, this is a huge reason as to why I care so much about empowering women and helping my clients. I feel blessed and grateful I had quality time with my son in the early years, but I knew I had to get back to work.

When Daniel turned three, the time was right, and I needed to get my purpose back beyond being mummy. I had Daniel and knew that I didn't want any more children. I felt guilty sitting at home bored and so it was time to look for a job.

He loved nursery and playing with other children.

"Mummy, please, can you pick me up later?" This was the question that greeted me every time I went to pick up my three-year-old son from nursery. I remember so vividly he stood there in his Bob the Builder outfit which he virtually lived in. We both began to thrive.

I enrolled at an agency and quickly got an interview as a receptionist for a company I knew nothing about. I will never forget the interview as the two people interviewing me were late, as they had been out the night before. They dashed in eventually, explaining how sorry they were. The interview went well and ended with, when can you start?

The nerves kicked in. Walking into the office the following Monday, I was confronted by two office assistants, who barely gave me a smile. All I needed to do was be my normal chirpy self and see if I liked it.

Financial Services was totally alien to me. I knew nothing about pensions, investments, mortgages – I just thought they were things that men dealt with.

I literally knew nothing but I enjoyed the office banter and they all seemed pleasant, but one thing struck me on that first day.

No woman advisers, only men! Why was that?

I took to the job quickly, answering the phone in my usual happy tone, photocopying, and generally enjoying having freedom and purpose again. At the end of each day, I was greeted by my happy little boy as I picked him up from nursery. If Daniel was happy that was all that mattered.

The days turned into weeks, and, as I settled in, it became apparent to me that I was working in a man's world. They were all middle aged, boring men, well, with a few exceptions. I quickly learned about what they all did, how they all earned their income and slowly financial services, pensions, investments, mortgages, life insurance didn't seem so boring.

Everyone that I was surrounded by was doing a job that I knew nothing about, and yet, the more I learned, the more I wanted to learn; I became addicted to learning.

From literally not knowing what any of these services were, I began soaking it all up like a sponge.

One morning when my boss George came into the office, I said, "Can I ask you? How do you become a financial adviser?" He told me that I would need to be qualified and pass many exams. My response was, "Okay, which exams and how do I go about it?"

He passed me a thick FPC manual with a hard purple cover. As it dropped onto the desk with a heavy bang, he said, "This is the first one."

For me, this was a turning point. I had found something for the first time that I was genuinely interested in. I soaked up the information and sat the first exam. I used the evenings to study whilst my son was in bed and my husband was working late.

I did this all on my own in my own time.

Learning on the job helped immensely. For the first time ever, I felt I had found my passion. I took my first exam nervously and passed. The feeling of seeing the certificate with my name on it spurred me onto the next exam. I felt for the first time, I could do it. Looking around at my colleagues, I felt inspired and determined to succeed and I knew that to succeed I had to continue to study, learn and progress.

I was addicted. I believed in myself for the first time. I knew I could do it – I was taking my place in a man's world, my way. All I needed was passion, sparkle and enthusiasm to make a dull subject of mortgages not seem so complex and boring.

There was a gentleman in the office called Martin Tolson, he was the number one adviser in the office at the time, and he became my mentor.

He said to me, one day, "I see you as a younger version of me, just remember people buy people, and you don't need to know everything. You just need to be able to get on with people. You can ask and find out what you don't know."

I never forgot that. He gave me my confidence and belief to keep going. Without him and his wise words and time he spent with me, I wouldn't be writing this.

By this time, I was thirty-six and fully qualified.

My mum sadly died at age 59, from cancer. This changed my perspective on life.

It gave me a different outlook. It makes you realise life is short. This is not a dress rehearsal, it's the real thing.

I had the qualifications, the knowledge, the skills but I still needed to do it for me rather than working for someone else.

Most of my colleagues had worked for banks, they already had clients, but I hadn't, so I made this conscious decision.

You have to start somewhere; I knew that if I found my clients it would enable me to follow my passion that would then allow me to travel and give me financial independence.

This was going to take time, and my motto is, 'If you believe in yourself you can do anything.'

So, I jumped from being an administrator with a salary to being a full-time self-employed Mortgage Adviser with no clients. I had to spread the word, and I had to do this asap as I had no income. I had to get out there and spread the word. Networking was the only way, so I set about finding some groups to go along to.

Six am starts aren't ideal but once I started there was no stopping me. My mantra was, 'The more people I can speak to the more people I can help.' Networking opened so many doors. It gave me confidence. I really felt I had found my way to freedom. I spoke passionately about my purpose, I felt on top of the world.

Once I got started, one mortgage led to another.

My version of success was unfolding. I had felt like a single mother whilst my husband was away working, totally trapped with no money. I began to build my business slowly, I was able to do life my way for my son and I, this feeling of being independent and smashing life regained my purpose. I felt like a social butterfly when I was out talking to people.

Juggling motherhood and work takes its toll, but as they grow up it allows you more time to concentrate on you. Daniel enjoyed school and as he got older this allowed me to work around his activities.

Daniel, my son, after his GCSEs, flew out to join his father in Australia. We had separated by this point, which was a tough time. I felt Australia was a good opportunity for him, and he was keen to go. I felt I had to let him go as I felt there were a lot of great opportunities for him, plus the sunshine of course.

My purpose of getting up every morning for the last sixteen years was no longer there.

I cried every day for six months.

I had to turn this negative into a positive, so I now had the time to focus on my business, working within an office environment had kept me focused, and I had to start to rebuild. My focus had been Daniel, as it had always been, but now it was to be able to afford to fly out for holidays. Divorce is always tough, but I had to keep going. No one was going to put a roof over my head. I had to do this. I had no choice. Work kept me going. I had juggled a career with so much devotion for my son, it was now time for me, so I put my head down and continued to build my clients within a business.

My mind was working overtime, with ideas and names whizzing around in my head. It just came to me, Miss

Moneypenny Mortgages, from nowhere. I instantly loved the name and smiled, very me, as I rushed home to Google the name to see if it had already been taken. To me, the name stood for my values and stood out as approachable and fun, now I felt I could be me.

Now I had the name. I just needed to get started. Nothing to hold me back now except myself. I dug deep and jumped, using all my strengths and skills I forgot I had hidden in my closet.

It has been six years now since Miss Moneypenny was born. From being a woman in a man's world for so long, I've been lucky to learn from some very knowledgeable, inspirational people, but it was now my turn.

I was a self-employed business owner, so I had the knowledge. I had been through a divorce. I had all the life skills. I knew exactly how to help business owners buy their dream home, and so I hit the ground running.

What makes me different? I would say I genuinely care and am not driven by money. Yes, we need to earn a living. But I have worked alongside so many target driven men who see pounds before people and, just recently, seen so many cases of bad advice, I know my clients get best advice.

My mentors said I have a special quality of, 'not being driven by money but being driven by helping people.'

I look back on the last twenty-five years and think, wow, I have come an awful long way. I drifted from leaving school to age thirty with lots of great achievements, Daniel being my greatest, at thirty. Walking into that job in financial services completely changed the course of my life for the better. I found my purpose after being financially dependent. This opportunity opened the door to me discovering Miss Moneypenny Mortgages – and becoming and doing life my way and showing everyone that they can do anything that a man can do, if they put their mind to it.

I want you to know that it is never too late to find your purpose and to follow your dream. I found my passion to help people and it's by doing it this way. I would have never thought I would be in this job. This is not about buying a house, it is about serving people and empowering them!

Spreading my knowledge to empower and educate is what I love doing at my own pace, which working for myself has enabled me to do. And if you love what you do, then it's not work. It's a passion.

Amanda's Business Gold

Top Tips to get Mortgage Ready

Check your Credit Score.

Be organised, we will need last three months bank statements and payslips so keep them safe.

Focus on reducing balances on credit cards.

Be sensible with 'buy now, pay later' credit.

Lenders don't like online betting, please avoid.

Don't worry if your credit isn't perfect, I can still help you.

Self-employed ideally need two years' income figures but I can help you if you only have one year's.

Know what you can borrow before you start looking, this way you will be in a more informed position.

Starting saving a small deposit can get you on the property ladder.

Speak to an expert – it will save you time and money.

POWERHOUSE

Rachael Hover

About the Author

Rachael Hover is a certified Digital Marketing Consultant and founder of RH Consultancy, with expertise in web design, paid ads, SEO, and strategic marketing.

With certifications from CDMP, Google, and Meta, and as a WIX Editor X Partner, she helps businesses grow their online presence and boost sales.

Rachael has consulted for several top UK and European corporations, leveraging her marketing and PRINCE2 project management skills to drive multi-million-pound initiatives.

Her passion is empowering ambitious entrepreneurs and corporate clients with tailored strategies that generate leads, increase visibility, and deliver results.

Backed by a skilled team, Rachael combines creativity and data-driven insights to help businesses scale online and offline.

Let's turn your vision into success.

Email: rachael@rachaelhover.com

Website: www.rachaelhover.com

Social media: www.instagram.com/rh_consultancy_/

Embrace Your Uniqueness

Right now, I am living a life that, not so long ago, was just a pipe dream, a selection of pictures I added to a vision board. I am running my own successful digital marketing consultancy, with a team of four, where I'm not answering to a boss because I am the boss.

No two days are the same, and that is one of the things I love so much about running my own business – the variety! One day, I could be working with a small business owner who is just starting out and has come to me to build their very first website, and the next day, I'm sitting in the boardroom of a multimillion-pound corporation strategising for their next paid marketing campaign.

My business, RH Consultancy, is a digital marketing consultancy. To put it simply, we help business owners 'get seen' and build their businesses through the power of marketing – more leads, more sales, and more clients! We specialise in four main areas: Website Design, SEO, Paid Advertising, and Social Media Marketing. We work with kitchen table businesses, multimillion-pound corporate businesses, and everything in between.

I sometimes have to pinch myself, realising that this is my life and that I get to do what I love for a living. Is every day great? No! Are there days when I've wanted to give it all up... Of course! Running a business is hard work and not for the faint-hearted!

But even on the toughest days (and there are quite a few) I remind myself that the alternative would be to work for someone else, to ask for time off, to ask for permission to take an hour out of my day to go to the dentist, and that is what drives me forward.

I wasn't always living this life though. Seven years ago, I was that person, and all I wanted was to escape, to be free from clocking in and out, to be in control of my own time, and to create a career and life that aligned with my passions.

Now, that vision has become my reality, and I feel more empowered than ever. With every project, I bring energy, creativity, and a unique perspective that my clients love. The freedom to shape my work and make decisions that drive real impact is exciting. It's not just about building websites, running campaigns, or delivering great results for my clients. It's about embracing my journey and the power that comes from knowing I've created a business from the ground up – one that gives me the flexibility and freedom I once only dreamed of.

I can still vividly remember that day, the day I ran down the street, tears streaming down my face as I was being chased by a girl in my year at school, my bully, and her older sister.

To this day I don't know how, as I wasn't the fastest runner! Being the overweight one, who hated PE, running was not my strong point, but I made it to my front door and got inside before they managed to get hold of me, I felt relief mixed with helplessness. But that wasn't the end of it; the bullying didn't stop. If anything, it intensified.

Things changed when my family moved, giving me a fresh start at a new school. But the damage was done. Once confident and outgoing, I became reserved and untrusting.

As the eldest daughter, I felt the weight of being a role model, a 'perfect' example. To cope, I became a people-pleaser which is something I still have to battle with today. Constantly trying to meet everyone's expectations while ignoring my own needs.

Food was a comfort, and with it came a struggle with my weight, which added to my self-doubt. Somewhere along the line, I began to believe them, feeling like I had to be perfect to be accepted, yet never feeling good enough.

As I got older, I was better at hiding how I felt, I became great at putting on a front. To look at me on the outside you would never have known any of this, I was the loudest, the seemingly confident one – but it was all a mask, a persona I wore to hide how unhappy I really was.

2012 was a turning point. After years of feeling massively unhappy with my weight and how it affected my confidence, I chose to undergo weight loss surgery. Over a period of four years, I lost over ten stone, and a new more confident me started to appear! Everything about me changed, not only my physical appearance but something inside me changed. I wanted more.

But this transformation has its own set of challenges. With my newfound confidence came unforeseen consequences – my thirteen-year relationship broke down. I wasn't the same person I was when we met, we wanted different things.

I remember the day when I decided to leave, I was thirty-two years old, standing on my parents' driveway with nothing but four bin bags full of clothes to my name. I had to start over. When friends were buying houses, getting married and having babies, I was single, living at my parents' house in my nephew's Thomas the Tank Engine decorated room. Terrified wasn't the word. I felt like a failure and questioned if I had made the right choice in turning my world upside down.

I threw myself into rebuilding my life, I rented my own apartment, got a better corporate job, and eventually met an incredible man who would later become my husband. But I still felt something was missing.

The entrepreneurial spirit I'd grown up with as both my parents ran their own successful businesses called – I didn't want to spend the next thirty years asking for holiday leave or waiting for Friday to come along so I could have two days a week that were my own. I craved the independence that only comes with being your own boss.

So, while working full-time, I started my first business, a handmade jewellery and gift business, I specialised in the wedding industry and created bespoke wedding favours. I worked all the hours to make it a success, evenings, weekends, even during my lunch break at my corporate job.

This business grew and out of this came my second business, an event planning business, planning and hosting wedding fairs in the Warwickshire and West Midlands area. I worked with local wedding venues and wedding suppliers organising wedding shows, and this business was also a success. At one point I was working full time in a corporate job, and running two businesses of my own; life was full on! It was from running my event planning business that my love of marketing emerged; it was a massive part of hosting a successful event. Due to the success of my events, suppliers in the wedding industry would ask me how I did it, and I would show them! And from this RH Consultancy was born.

Then, the world changed. COVID-19 hit and forced us all to work from home, but I saw this as a massive opportunity to focus more on my business. And it thrived! When we were told to return to the office, I knew it was time… I didn't want to go back!

So, I took the leap, I handed in my notice. Leaving my job, despite at this stage only having a small but loyal client base, was a mix of terror and excitement! My husband was so supportive and encouraged me to take the leap, and I set a goal: if I could match my corporate salary, I'd consider it a success.

Today, I'm not just matching it – I'm quadrupling it. The journey wasn't without challenges, but it taught me resilience, self-belief, and the power of pursuing what truly matters. Building this business was never just about financial freedom; it was about building a life on my terms.

I have had to deal with some pretty bad online bullying, people talking about me behind my back, as well as challenges building my team! I made some errors in the hiring process and hired the wrong people in the beginning who were detrimental to my company rather than helping it grow, but looking back they are all events that helped shape who I am today.

To anyone wondering if they're ready for change or capable of more, I assure you – you are. Sometimes, all it takes is one bold decision to uncover the Powerhouse that's hiding beneath the surface!

Rachael's Business Gold

I've learned that no one succeeds alone. My husband has been my biggest fan. I cannot thank him enough for being that support and strength, but also finding a community of like-minded business owners has been invaluable.

Through masterminds and business communities, I connected with people who understand the highs and lows of entrepreneurship. They've celebrated my wins, supported me through setbacks, and become lifelong friends. Surrounding yourself with those who 'get it' is invaluable.

Running and growing a business taught me resilience, the kind that pushes you forward even when it's tempting to stay in bed. When you are solely responsible for whether your mortgage is paid… you get out of bed! No sick pay here!

I learned the value of accountability – not just for clients, but for myself – and, crucially, that who I am is enough.

It's a message I pass on to my clients: you are your biggest asset. No one else can replicate your story, voice, or passion. If you don't believe in yourself, no one else will.

My golden rule is simple: embrace your uniqueness and let it shine in everything you do. This mindset not only attracts the right clients but also makes work truly fulfilling.

Everyone starts somewhere, and, often, that place feels far from powerful. But it's in moments when we feel everything is against us and that it can't get any worse, that we uncover our true strength.

POWERHOUSE

Lindsey Fairhurst

About the Author

Lindsey Fairhurst's career as an Executive Personal Assistant spans 23 years. She is a serial planner and organiser and has a passion for providing innovative and strategic solutions with drive and enthusiasm.

Her clients have been UHNWI (Ultimate High Net Worth Individuals), six-figure earners, and best-selling authors, and she has been featured in leading publications. In the corporate world, she has supported Senior Executives and C-suite teams within multi-national companies.

Lindsey coaches women to transition from corporate roles into working for themselves, elevating their lives with her SHE ELEVATES programme – the ultimate goal-setting and accountability experience.

Utilising their unique skills and career history, she successfully mentors and teaches them how to set up and launch businesses that offer an independent location lifestyle. She empowers her clients to use their skills and attributes, together with the tools and knowledge she shares, to create the perfect business foundation offering flexibility and a five-figure income, without them having to leave the house.

Lindsey sees each day as a new experience. When she is not working you will find her out in the Dubai sunshine, wakesurfing at sea, cycling in the desert, in the gym, or lounging at the most sought-after Dubai hot spots.

She loves to travel which is why she created an online business where she can work when required which gives her an independent location lifestyle.

On her bucket list for 2025 is to go scuba diving in the Maldives, ride the world's longest zipline, and take a hot air balloon over the desert in Dubai.

Welcome on this journey, hold tight it's going to be exciting!

Email: lindsey@lindseyfairhurst.com

Website: www.lindseyfairhurst.com

Social media: www.instagram.com/thevirtual_assistant/

Live Life by DESIGN, Not Default

In a world where nothing changes, nothing changes. This is a realisation I had many years ago when working in a corporate role in 2017. Had I not thought strategically, really looked at what I wanted, invested in coaching support, and made changes to my daily routine, I would not be living in our dream villa in Dubai. We created the ultimate work-from-home outdoor living space, complete with a swimming pool. It truly is the dream!

We moved to Dubai in August 2015 with £30k, which went within six months. To date, our assets total over a half million pounds. We made that happen.

Reflection and being open to growth over the years have catalysed my journey. I feel truly blessed to have had the support from those around me, courage, tenacity, grit, and determination to keep moving forward despite challenges and obstacles.

Having discipline and living by my EPIC formula has supported me in reaching my goals, and I am here to share how that can work for you too.

If you want accountability to take your life and business to the next level, read on.

In October 2017, I worked as an Executive Assistant to a Chief Operation Officer based in the financial district of Dubai. A high-profile financial investment company, I was on the highest salary I had ever received, and the role had excellent benefits.

After being made redundant only a few months prior, I had gone into this role fired up and ready for a new challenge and career progression. Three months into the job I felt miserable, unappreciated, and lost. I was clashing with the Chief Operation Officer, we were not aligned, and I found myself in unknown territory.

After some reflection, I realised the role was not for me and decided it was best to leave. The kicker here was the Chief Operation Officer felt the same way about me leaving. My confidence was at an all-time low.

In a six-month period, I was made redundant, walked out of a job, we moved house, and I had to undergo tests for breast cancer due to a lump I found. Dubai life certainly was not sparkling!

During this time, I wanted to go back home to England. It felt tough; I had lost my sparkle, but I knew running away was not the answer. Especially as my husband had just invested £10k of our savings in a trade license to set up his sports management business, specialising in football for expats.

I spent time reflecting on what I wanted my future to look like. I wanted to, 'Live Life by Design, not Default,' have a career I was fulfilled in, and create an online business that would allow me to have an independent location lifestyle.

I got to work, did the research, and set up as a Virtual Personal Assistant, supporting businesses and individuals remotely regardless of where they were in the world.

Setting up a business was challenging. It was tough. I wondered if it would get me to my goal. Imposter syndrome kicked in. Could I do this?

I launched my website and business services in January 2018 with a handful of clients. I became fully booked quite quickly, enabling me to outsource to other women and work collectively.

I found so many benefits to working for myself. I could set my hours, find the clients I wanted to work with and align with them. I could work from any location in the world. I had flexibility and could travel. I set my pay rates, increased my confidence, and became my own boss.

One thing I missed was the in-person people connection. Instead of seeing this as a challenge, I looked to diversify and reached out to local agencies in Dubai to see if any part-time hybrid administration roles were available. Temporary and part-time roles were available, and this was a catalyst for change for me. I could do both. I viewed the temporary part-time Dubai roles as projects and worked with my clients on this. It was MAGIC!

Throughout 2018-19, I lived by my motto, 'Live life by Design, not Default.' Life felt great again.

Enter COVID-19, a time that changed lives forever, a time when I realised the power of having my own online flexible business.

Before we went into lockdown in Dubai, I was working a full-time temporary contract as an Executive PA. I also had one client of my own that paid me for ten hours a month. This ticked the boxes for me from a financial and personal perspective.

I had been working like this for a few years and it was a great balance. I always knew online and hybrid working would be the future, so when I set up as a Virtual PA I felt I was getting ahead of the game! COVID accelerated the online world of people working from home.

The contract that I had through corporate ended immediately; all temp staff were served notice. My husband's business stopped dramatically because no sporting games were allowed with COVID. We found ourselves in a position with no income. We had to diversify. I am not saying we were the only ones in turmoil; people were affected in many ways.

We had never been in a position with no income coming in, and being unable to leave the house made this all the more worrying.

Having been in similar positions, I immediately ramped up my online virtual assistance presence. I created an outreach strategy and plugged myself into online forums and Facebook groups. This worked; the clients signed, my diary was filled, and the income came. I was working eighteen-hour days due to the contracts that I took on to support women in business.

Like most, we went through the lockdown nervous and hopeful that life would resume. It was mentally challenging for my husband, after building a football business for four years, to see it crashing in front of him. We received no government funding or financial support for the business, it was all on us.

At the time of COVID-19 we lived in an apartment block. What many people will not know is that we advertised in the Facebook groups to clean cars in the car park basement for cash exchange. One day we found ourselves cleaning a red Ferrari 488 GTB in the basement car park for £20. We did it for our sanity and to get out of the apartment.

We look back and laugh about this now. It was a time we fought hard and did what we needed to survive.

Throughout 2020 and into 2021 we both worked for ourselves. We worked hard, enjoyed life, and built the businesses. We had a dream to buy our first property in Dubai and set about the strategy to save for the deposit.

My business was booming. I worked to develop myself and learn what was required for a successful business and to look after my clients, implementing processes and structure to my day.

My focus was on my clients, and I found time would slip away quite easily. Some days I would be in my home office for ten hours but only time tracking for six to seven hours. Losing time when working for yourself is like seeing money slide away.

I adapted to the work-from-home routine but missed people connection and I was not exercising enough. To help me become more accountable, I signed up with a coach to get more out of my day. I found working for myself could be a bit lonely, and having a buddy at the end of WhatsApp and weekly calls for support worked for me.

The accountability programme I joined honestly changed my life. I worked with Ange for four months and, we completely reworked my morning routine. I was firing on all cylinders by 9am. Between the hours of 6am and 9am I would work through a list of items which supported my mental, fitness and wellbeing. I was looking after myself each day before I went online to look after my clients.

It was, and still is, very important to me to feel motivated, and this is not something you can switch on and off. I learnt that motivation comes from doing and being consistent. This is not easy but if you have a plan and are committed to your daily routine, it feeds into achieving goals in the bigger picture. This is something I am very passionate about.

Having lived and breathed my success as a Virtual PA I felt passionate about others doing the same. I created a training programme to support other women who wanted to set up for themselves. The Virtual Assistant Academy programme opens twice a year and has done so since 2020. I also coach and mentor women on a one-to-one basis to achieve this business model set-up.

It has given me so much over the years and I love to see others create their life by design, not default. No one wants to stay in a job they don't like. Having flexibility is a game changer.

In the summer of 2021, it was time for me to step back into full-time employment to enable us to get all the official documentation to apply for a mortgage in Dubai.

I worked for an oil company for a high-net-worth individual as his office manager. It wasn't necessarily something I wanted to do. It didn't give me the get-up and go in a full-time role, but it was just something that I had to do at the time.

Thinking of the bigger picture, a new home, another property for us, a place to settle so we don't have to move again, a garden project to create the ultimate work-from-home space. I saw it as a short-term sacrifice for long-term gain.

Having a goal or a dream or wanting to make changes within your life must start somewhere. It starts with YOU! It starts with having a 'can do, will do, I can' attitude.

This comes from feeding yourself the right things. I am not talking just about food. I'm talking about what you read and listen to, and your financial investment in yourself for coaching, mentoring, or counselling if required. Your exercise, morning routine, evening routine, blocking out the noise, and putting yourself first – doing what it takes to get you where you want to be.

Once I realised it was on me to create the life I craved, I felt empowered and uplifted. No one is here to do it for you. You need to take control and, more importantly, take action.

When I reflect, I am a little mind-blown by what we have achieved in nine years in Dubai. It is all due to work ethic, reflection, being open to growth, and investment.

For me, the biggest realisation is seeing change as redirection, not rejection.

In nine years, we moved to a new country and set up a life. We moved house six more times. I worked on eight corporate contracts, walked out of one of those roles and was made redundant from two. I set up my own Virtual PA business, finding clients that give me an income upwards of

£4K per month. I created a VA training programme to share with other women so they could also change their lives. We bought a property in Dubai and renovated the outdoor living space to create an Ibiza-inspired sanctuary. On top of all of this, I have had other personal challenges, as we all do, and the hard-hitting recent news that my journey to becoming a mother is not so straightforward.

I would never have been able to achieve all I have without the support of others in my life. Some as an investment in them and myself to progress. Others who I choose to have in my life as they lift me and fill my cup; my friends, family, and husband.

Has my journey been easy? No! In the past five years, I have invested in myself, courses, coaches and mentors that each served a purpose: accountability, time, support or guidance. Some days, a general talk to help me get my thoughts straight.

My business coach, Helen McCue, supported me with the launch and planning of the VA Academy four years ago. That programme has changed many women's lives and will continue to do so.

I attended mindset therapy to support entering a new decade of my life and the challenges that have come with that.

My accountability coach taught me so much in such a short space of time. Years on, I still implement the routine we developed along with my fitness and wellbeing daily routine with my Personal Trainer, Natalie Ellis.

I use tracking to keep myself focused and moving forward. I have a Fitness Pal to track my food when I want to cut back and revert to my previous meal plans and exercise plans from my PT.

I use habit trackers for finance and day-to-day habits to ensure I am recording statistics for progress.

I use a 90-day planner system to help me break my year down and see the key focus points each month.

I have learned to reflect more and use a brain dump to give me a clear headspace.

A solid, effective morning routine is essential, as it gets me organised and in the right headspace for the day.

I always have a word of the year. My 2023 word was EPIC, which translates to:

"If you know the PURPOSE and are INTENTIONAL about the CONSISTENCY, the EXPERIENCE will be worth it."

It was a word that had a deep meaning for me. I connected to it.

My 2024 word of the year was ELEVATE; it was very impactful as I chose to be part of the POWERHOUSE Book collaboration, bringing me to you, the reader.

It also links into my new accountability program. SHE ELEVATES: The ultimate goal setting and accountability experience to support your growth and personal development, which launched in January 2025.

Lindsey's Business Gold

If nothing changes, nothing changes. I would love you to think about your life and how you want it to be. What needs to change for you to ELEVATE and live your life by design, not by default?

- You can think about it.
- You can procrastinate.
- You can make notes.
- You can speak to people.
- You can read.
- You can listen to inspirational podcasts.

However, unless you take action and create a plan with strategic steps, you will most likely feel stuck and stay exactly where you are. That is not what I want for you for 2025 and beyond.

Life is a journey on which we are all on to succeed. I believe in having the right people by your side to get you where you want to be.

My message is don't struggle to follow through and achieve your goals.

If you are lacking clarity, create a clear action plan. Be specific, measurable, achievable, relevant, and time bound.

If you fear failure, reframe it as a learning opportunity. Embrace a growth mindset by focusing on progress rather than perfection.

If overwhelm gets to you, prioritise goals and break them into smaller steps. Focus on one task at a time.

If you have an insufficient accountability framework and find completing things tough, consider joining an accountability group or finding an accountability partner.

I have the experience, mindset and processes to hold myself accountable. Now it is time to share how YOU can do the same and change YOUR LIFE, one day at a time. I have created a 6-week programme, which I am incredibly excited to share with you. You can find more information by heading over to www.lindseyfairhurst.com/sheelevates/

I have a lot to give – welcome on this journey; hold tight, it will be exciting!

Wishing you success in 2025 and beyond.

Lindsey Fairhurst – The woman who lives life by DESIGN, not default.

POWERHOUSE

Louisa Herridge

About the Author

Louisa Herridge is a four-time best-selling author and TEDx Speaker. She is a passionate and empowering writing coach who inspires and supports women to find their own power and success through using their story in business content, book collaborations and writing their own best-selling books.

Louisa does this by helping women to build their businesses by using her 'Storytelling for Success' method to create inspiring and authentic content by tapping into their meaning and purpose and using their story as a superpower to connect with their ideal clients.

Louisa also leads The Publishing Pod alongside her partner Jo Wildsmith, and works with authors to support them in planning, writing, editing, and publishing their business non-fiction books.

Email: hello@louisaherridge.co.uk

Website: www.louisaherridge.co.uk

Social media: www.instagram.com/louisa_herridge

On the Other Side of Fear

I first stuck a dream onto a vision board in 2020, just before lockdown and the months of change that turned life on its head. I was new to the world of self-development, and it felt like a game as I cut out photos from a magazine. I was a teacher struggling with anxiety and depression, juggling teaching with being a solo mum to a four-year-old, dealing with the aftermath of an abusive relationship and living with PTSD.

Now, four years later, I know that every time I put something onto a vision board or write down a goal I am doing so with intention and determination to succeed. Just this month I have paid off two holidays that have been on my vision board for the last two years – Walt Disney World Florida and a family seven-night cruise to Norway booked for my dad's 70th. You see this is my version of success. I am not one for designer clothes, handbags, or fancy cars – my love language is holidays. (But I did finally buy a new car this year too!) This Christmas I took Emilie to Lapland UK – one of our many adventures together. This trip meant that I had achieved another goal – to have travelled somewhere away from home in each school holiday of the year!

When I left teaching four years ago to start my own business, I had a version of success that I wanted to achieve. It wasn't centred around the number of zeros at the end of my pay cheque, it was about time and experiences. You see as a teacher for sixteen years I had all the holiday time but what I didn't have was freedom. I didn't have the freedom to take my daughter to school on her first day or to cheer her on at sports day. For nearly two decades I nurtured other people's children, but when it came to my own it was expected that I would sacrifice her needs. Emilie's first three months at school were the worst three months. In that time as well as coping as a working mum, I was going through a family court trial, she had scarlet fever and a vomiting bug, and to top it all off we had an OFSTED inspection. By Christmas 2019 I was on the floor. Signed off sick with anxiety and depression and feeling broken in every sense of the word.

Lockdown brought me the time away from school to be a mum again and time to begin healing along with the chance to set myself some new goals. I used this time to retrain, and this started my venture into self-employment.

But the last four years haven't been easy. Leaving a profession and starting a business is not the overnight success that many people would like you to believe it is. In fact, the infamous third year in business which is often known as the 'make or break' year, did in fact nearly break me. I had overspent by trying to 'keep up the appearances' of success from fancy retreats, holidays, hair extensions and signing up to every shiny course going – eventually 'faking it until you make it' hit me slap in the face.

You see – ambition, knowledge and determination can only get you so far, especially when anxiety, depression and PTSD are lurking beneath the surface, and in spite of my business wins, I felt like I was failing, and the guilt was huge. Having already hit rock bottom in 2019 and publicly showcasing my business growth, I felt somewhat of a fraud to start telling people again that things were shit. But they were. I was haemorrhaging money from the business; I owed people money and my personal spending had crept up so high that I was again sinking in the quicksand of debt.

2023 I was a mess. PTSD nightmares were nightly, and triggers were around constantly. I felt such a fraud as to the outside world I portrayed that I was thriving in my business but in reality, I was spending days on end lying on the sofa, crying more than I wanted to admit, with no real plan for the business.

I'd pivoted from teacher to coach and along the way had written three books. Without even meaning to, writing had taken over as my true purpose and I felt conflicted within the business. As a way to earn money alongside growing the business, I had been working freelance with two business owners that I highly respected and wanted to emulate. I was proofreading business books, writing media bios, press releases and all of this gave me great experience of working with clients from a range of businesses. However, the more I spent time proofreading and writing, the more diluted my own messaging became.

In 2022, I paid £10K to join a Positive Psychology coaching course, believing that the missing piece was that I needed a coaching qualification. It wasn't. I was already a good teacher and coach, but I just wasn't following my true purpose. I don't regret the course as I learned so much but when it came to launching and selling my course as a newly branded 'Positive Psychology course' I just felt like a phoney. Not only was the work I was trying to sell not 100% lighting me up, I also felt a HUGE FRAUD. I was promoting myself as a 'Wellbeing and Happiness' expert but on the inside, I was back to square one of anxiety and depression. My mental health was suffering due to another long, drawn-out family court battle which had had a huge knock-on effect on Emilie.

What the Positive Psychology course did introduce me to was what was to become my signature method, 'Storytelling for Success' and the more I used this with clients, the more drawn I came to storytelling and writing. My two book collaborations started off as passion projects and although I did earn money from them, they were not part of any business strategy. After launching my own book in 2021, I had a calling to bring together a group of women to share their stories. Like a magnet, I was naturally attracting women who had been through adversity and being so open with my own story had inspired others.

Volume 1 was a huge success and then came further success with Volume 2.

During a mastermind I remember the coach asking me what my true passion and purpose was. My gut knew the answer. But there were other far more established people than me publishing books and from a tech perspective I just didn't have a clue. Out of everything that I was selling and promoting, it was the book collaborations that were lighting me up. Deep down I knew that I wanted to carry on writing and helping people to publish, after all being an author had always been my one true ambition in life. I grew up wanting to be an author, and after finishing my English degree, took a master's in television and radio scriptwriting and when I trained to be an English teacher, my promise to myself was that I would use the holidays to write a book. My novel has been started and this is still my ultimate goal… watch this space.

At the end of 2022 I started working with a new business coach and she was the first person that I opened up to about my spiralling debts. I owed £10K for the book collaboration, had another £10K plus on a loan and had maxed out personal credit cards paying off courses and masterminds. I didn't have a strategy and my mental health was spiralling.

'Stop the Spend.' That was the mantra for 2023. She made me write down everything that I owed, and which were my priority. I had already started selling book collaboration number three, but I was in a catch-22. My mental health was so bad that I couldn't actively sell, but if I didn't sell then I couldn't pay back the business debt that I owed and in amongst all of this I was still claiming Universal Credit which was keeping me small. I couldn't earn more than £2K a month without feeling that I was losing out. So, I needed a circuit break. What was the point of having a big house and a social media that 'looked' like I had it all when inside I was crumbling and my business was no longer lighting me up?

It was time to go back to teaching. This is what my family told me, this is what my depression told me, and I nearly listened. I signed up to teaching supply agencies. I cancelled my book collaboration and gave people their money back which left me skinter than ever. I pulled my head out of the sand. It was time to make a plan and stop winging it in business.

I started therapy and during nineteen sessions over six months I found the answers to so many things personally and for the business. I didn't have to go back to teaching... I had another plan.

I decided to significantly downsize my home, to stop the spend and to back myself. By moving to a much smaller home reducing my outgoings by half I was able to close my Universal Credit claim. I had two months with absolutely no money and family had to help me out, but I stepped into my new era. During therapy I was able to address my fears, my procrastination and self-sabotage and the answer to my problems became obvious.

Enter The Publishing Pod.

I was hiding. I was whispering my ideas for what I really wanted to do in my business.

While money pressure had reduced, it was the perfect time to be brave. The only thing stopping me was fear, but my therapist and new CBT techniques helped me to step through this.

Recently, watching 'Rob and Romesh Versus Stunts' as they were set on fire, they were reminded of the mantra… "On the other side of fear is everything that you want." I knew deep down what I wanted, and it was time. I also had reached the stage where people were associating me with books and writing, and people were coming to me and asking me to work with them. It was a no-brainer.

One of the best thing that has come out of starting my business is the incredible friends that I have made and one of these key friendships is with Jo Wildsmith. Jo and I had discussed publishing together six months earlier; she wanted to work with me to publish my collaboration, but I had already started to take sign-ups for Volume 3 and felt stuck. I wanted to be loyal to the other publisher, but I had been spending thousands to publish my books with them when I had all the tools, skills, and connections to create my own business by publishing with Jo. We both had the same business mentor who helped me to work through a business plan and to finally put strategy into my business.

I also had an author from one of my collaborations, Paula Poppy, who wanted to write a book and, in her words, "I only want to do it with you." She became our 'guinea pig' and together we tip-toed into the world of publishing. I was an experienced writer, editor and proof-reader and Jo knew all the stuff that I had no interest in learning. Together we became the perfect team with our mission being to help people to publish with 'passion and precision.' Paula successfully published her book in March 2024, and it was a huge success.

Soon after, Dawn Gadsby signed up to write a book with us. I also had six authors signed up to write in my all-new collaboration, but I was scared. Scared of what people were saying about me. Feeling guilty about the mistakes I'd made and people I'd upset. Apologetic about wanting to run a business doing the thing that I am really fucking good, qualified in and SO passionate about.

I knew that I had been keeping myself small but knowing deep inside that I had SO much more. Throughout 2023 I worked steadily and paid off the business debt and put plans in place to pay off the personal debt. It was hard. I was so skint that I couldn't afford to go on holiday and at Christmas, my sister helped me to buy presents. My mum and brother lent me money and it felt like the longest year ever. But I did it. I paid off the debt and so by the time our first book was launched in 2024, I was not indebted to anyone. I felt free.

As a writing coach, I wanted to step into my authority and be known for 'Storytelling for Success' as a tool to help entrepreneurs to connect their story to their business. The stronger that my mind became from therapy and as my anxiety and depression lessened, the more confident and determined I felt in business. I was aligned with what I was doing, and I knew that I was the expert. For the first time I fully leant into being THE go-to person and it was time to step back up a level and get visible.

In November 2023, I delivered a TEDx talk and spoke about the power of reading and how I believe that reading can change the world. Within this talk, I also shared my story. I have shared my story many times, but this time it was different. There was no longer that little niggle in me that needed my story to be heard so that I was believed, so that I looked strong or that I looked healed. I shared a snippet of my story because I was in my power, and I knew that someone needed to hear it. Someone needed to know that I had come back from the brink and had healed. When I share my story now, I know that my story is no longer about me, it is about whoever needs to hear it and that is the true superpower of 'Storytelling for Success.' I am now in charge of how I interpret and tell my story and therein lies the power. This was what I would now be known for!

In January 2024, I promised myself that I was going to get known for 'Storytelling for Success' and would speak on multiple stages! I did it. I rebranded as Louisa Herridge Limited in April 2024 and launched my collaboration to great success.

We supported four authors to self-publish and ended the year with ten authors booked in to publish over the year. I also leaned into the niche that I really wanted to pursue – collaborations. I want to be known as the go-to person for book collaborations, like this one, to create business opportunities for other entrepreneurs to lead their own and bring this incredible opportunity to their network. I now have a waiting list for business collaborations as I am booked up into 2026!

In September at the launch of 'She Empowers' collaboration, with Niki Kinsella, I snapped an arrow with my throat. It changed my life and from that moment I stepped fully onto the other side of fear.

I have stopped being afraid. I have fully stepped into my power, and I am no longer afraid to be known as the expert in storytelling, writing and connecting YOU to your business in publishing your business book.

I knew the arrow break was going to be hard and I'd heard how empowering it could be, but I had no clue on the impact it would have.

We were asked to set an intention or a fear that we wanted to break as we broke the arrow. I knew what I wanted to break but struggled to find the words.

As I stood placing the arrow on the soft part of my throat I was consumed with fear. Not of the arrow hurting me, but of facing the thing that holds me back. Fear of being loved again. Fear of allowing myself to love. Fear of even trusting myself to love. Fear of being enough.

As I leant into the arrow, the very real vision of my ex flooded my brain. His face, the one that is ingrained in my memory and for a long time haunted me in nightmares and flashbacks.

Thanks to therapy he doesn't live in my head anymore but in that moment he was there. As I felt the pressure of the arrow burrow into my neck and felt the intensity increase, so did my determination and my power. My head was a sea of red and my sole purpose to break that arrow and be free of him.

When it broke his face was instantly gone. A white euphoric light filled my head and the joy I felt was a moment I won't forget. The tears flowed and Niki scooped me up.

Afterwards I could feel the part of my throat where the arrow had been. Also, the part that has been a trigger for five years, always reminding me of his hands on my throat during the assault.

Now when I touch my throat, I only feel power.

I'm on the other side of that fear and I feel like I shed a skin.

People noticed a change in me over the following weeks and months and I felt a huge shift in the business.

I began working to refine my offers and pricing and everything felt different. I am finding sales easy because the difference is I am selling what I love. I am selling what I know I am the expert in, and my passion cannot be hidden! This is what I am meant to be doing! As I was told right at the start of my business journey 'Profit follows passion.'

At the end of 2024, I welcomed more new authors into my world and doubled last year's revenue and have recurring revenue through until the end of 2025.

I am so excited to launch my new 'Write with Me' container this year that will help so many others to connect to their story and write their dream book! And to continue to enhance and create collaboration experiences including my first Writing Retreat.

It's time to get loud, to stop whispering and to set big scary goals that excite me. I no longer have to cope with the white noise of fear, but I wouldn't be where I am now if I hadn't hit the rock-bottom of 2019 and again in 2023.

Success is not a straight line and so for my business gold I want to leave you with this:

Louisa's Business Gold

Who decided that I'm good enough?

Liz asked in her opening chapter what makes us a Powerhouse? I know that I am a Powerhouse, but it has taken time for me to be able to step fully into that notion.

I didn't aways believe I was good enough but…

When I didn't think anyone would pay £150 to work with me, five people signed up for my first course.

When I didn't think, anyone would pay to do a Book Collaboration with me, they did… and they paid me… twenty-eight times to be precise…

When I didn't think people would pay extra to work one-to-one with me so that I could help to pull out the true power of their stories, they did.

When I didn't think people would pay to spend the day with me to work on their mindset, business and creative ideas, they did and then they came back again… and again.

When I didn't think anyone would want me to proof edit their entire book and pay me for my advice and expertise, they did… and then they recommended me to other people.

When I didn't think a Powerhouse entrepreneur would say YES to working with me to bring together their own tribe of authors to create something magical, they did.

So, who decided that I am good enough? Who decides that you are good enough to do what you want to do?

If you struggle with that belief, then look at the evidence in front of you. It is not up to us to prove we are good enough; it is the people that put the trust in us and our expertise that show we ARE good enough. So, until you can believe yourself, believe the people around you.

I am so grateful to the many clients who trusted me even when I was trying to trick myself into believing that I wasn't good enough.

We are ALL good enough.

Printed in Great Britain
by Amazon